MW01205101

RESCUED

Chronicles of the Call:
Book One

Marigold Cheshier

Firewind Ministries

RESCUED: Chronicles of the Call: Book One
By Marigold Cheshier

Firewind Ministries
1218 Oakhill Road
Ozark, MO 65721

ISBN: 978-1-939565-01-3

Copyright © 2013 by Marigold Cheshier
All rights reserved

Cover designed by Shereen Cheshier
All rights reserved

Scriptures marked KJV are taken from the KING JAMES VERSION (KJV): KING JAMES VERSION, public domain.

Scriptures marked NASB are taken from the NEW AMERICAN STANDARD BIBLE (NASB): Scripture taken from the NEW AMERICAN STANDARD BIBLE ®, Copyright © 1960, 1962, 1963, 1968, 1971, 1972, 1973, 1975, 1977, 1995 by The Lockman Foundation. Used by permission.

Scriptures marked NASU are taken from the NEW AMERICAN STANDARD UPDATED (NASU): Scripture taken from the NEW AMERICAN STANDARD UPDATED BIBLE ®, copyright ©, 1995 by The Lockman Foundation. Used by permission.

Scriptures marked NIV are taken from the NEW INTERNATIONAL VERSION (NIV): Scripture taken from THE HOLY BIBLE, NEW INTERNATIONAL VERSION ®. Copyright © 1973, 1978, 1984, 2011 by Biblica, Inc.TM. Used by permission of Zondervan.

Scriptures marked NLT are taken from the HOLY BIBLE, NEW LIVING TRANSLATION (NLT): Scriptures taken from the HOLY BIBLE, NEW LIVING TRANSLATION, Copyright © 1996, 2004, 2007 by Tyndale House Foundation. Used by permission of Tyndale House Publishers, Inc., Carol Stream, Illinois 60188. All rights reserved. Used by permission.

DEDICATION

I dedicate this volume of **Chronicles of the Call** and the many that follow to my wonderful, supportive family: my husband of 47 years, Mike Cheshier; my firstborn Melissa Cheshier White; my last born, James Michael Cheshier; and my wonderful grandchildren Michael and Maurice White and Serenity and Gabriel Cheshier. Also, in memory of my dedicated-to-the-cause Mother and Daddy, James and Juanita Allen; and my only sister and her husband, Marcia and Maurice Lednicky.

Dedicated to the Lover of my soul, Jesus Christ of Nazareth, the Son of the living God, Yeshua, Yahweh, Emmanuel, the One who has given me life.

But most of all:

In loving dedication to

The LION OF THE TRIBE OF JUDAH

ACKNOWLEDGEMENTS

My special heartfelt thanks to the many friends and colleagues that have encouraged me to write. There are so many to whom I am indebted. Without you, this would not have happened.

Thank you, Jane Sullivan. She rarely heard one of my stories that she didn't tell me to write it down. Even though she has gone on to her eternal reward, I can still feel her pushing me on.

Thanks to a great, extraordinary friend and colleague, Lori Loomis, who is not only an inspiration to me, but was willing to pre-read all my work. She is a gifted and talented woman of God, speaker, and writer. When I feel overwhelmed, she seems to radar in on my condition and makes herself available to assist me in any way possible. Everyone should have a friend like Lori. I simply could not have done this project without her. Lori is also responsible for the layout of this book. You're wonderful. Contact: *loomisrl@windstream.net*

Thanks to a wonderful editor, Majetta Morris at: Majetta Morris, Free Lance Editor, Bright Light Editing *mailto:majettamorris@yahoo.com. Majetta came into my life at just the right time, God's perfect time, and has become a dear friend. I met Majetta* when I was the guest speaker for a statewide ladies' conference. I was nearly finished writing and thought the remainder of the work would be a walk in the park. Man, was I wrong! Majetta has shown me the way. She is gifted, precious, and exciting to work with. I enjoy brainstorming with her. This is just the beginning of our relationship. You're a dear!

Thanks to the cover graphic design artist, Shereen Cheshier, my daughter-in-law, for her dedication to the artwork. She is a talented artist, and we are blessed to have her as part of this team. She is a gifted designer. Love you, girl! Contact Shereen at mikeyandshereen @hotmail.com.

One year ago, I fractured my ribs just before flying off to Africa. Once I arrived in the bush, I could not leave because the ribs had re-fractured from the rough roads. Terri Magness, a dear friend scheduled to be in Africa for only two weeks, changed her flight schedule and stayed in the bush with me for a month to keep me company. Terri, a talented writer in her own rights with a couple of published books, thought she could use the quiet time to write. On her first day with me she said, "Marigold, it's time you get down to business and write. I am here to see that you do just that." Thanks Terri, you're the best.

Thanks for believing in me and pushing me forward.

A huge thanks to my loving devoted husband, Mike, who has endured hours of alone time while I write. He doesn't complain about my constant "what do you think" questions. Mike, I could never have written a word without your support. Mike is my sweetheart, my biggest fan who eagerly reads everything to make sure that I stay on track. I am so blessed to have such a great life-partner.

Thanks to my family, all of them—son, daughter, grandkids, daughter-in-law, and son-in-law—who have played a part in this book. They have encouraged me, prayed with me, added their spin, and caused the writing to be fun. The eighteen-year-old twins, while in Africa over the summer, reminded me of things about which I should write. They are awesome. Serenity, my five-year-old granddaughter, is forever asking me to tell her stories of my adventures in Africa. I must say a big thanks to Mikey Cheshier, my son, who carefully read every word and added his perspective to the stories. He is a very gifted writer. My daughter, Melissa White, has been a source of strength and encouragement throughout the entire project. My sister and brother-in-law, Marcia and Maurice Lednicky, have been prayer partners and confidants. I am blessed and grateful for a supportive, incredible family. You have made this possible.

My friends and prayer partners—God bless you, and thanks so much for letting me whine when things didn't seem to go as planned. Also, thank you Marcia Lednicky, Ruby Hoke, Jean Rogers, Melissa White, Lori Loomis, Stephanie Domengeaux, and many more who I call regularly for prayer. God bless you!

A huge thanks to all the women that have been in my services and requested these stories in writing. To you I owe a debt of gratitude. Without you, I would not have written one word. I love you. Thank you for loving me.

And last, but certainly not least, thanks to the Great I AM! The One that Was, and Is, and Is To Come! The Lion of the Tribe of Judah! My Deliverer out of Zion! The Nazarene! Jesus, the Son of God. You are the story. Without You, there would be nothing worth writing. Thank You, Father, Son, and Holy Spirit.

I love you all!

Marigold Cheshier

TABLE OF CONTENTS

FOREWORD

RUINED FOR THE ORDINARY

Truth is stranger than fiction, and the words written within the pages of this book are true even though at times they seem unbelievable.

Upon reflection of the life God has privileged me to live, I discovered that very little has been what most people would consider "normal." What is "normal" anyway?

When considering how to share all God has led me through in this extraordinary journey—from my personal testimonies of miracles and healings through all the travels in ministry—I found that I could never separate all these things. The story would be incomplete if I did. So, I'm including the whole God-ordained journey.

My parents, James and Juanita Allen, pastors at Bastrop, Louisiana, taught me to love Jesus with all my heart, mind, body, and soul. I believe I knew at a very early age I was called to preach as I recall preaching to my dolls and spanking them when they didn't live right. I remember doing this, so I may have been a little older; however, Mom said I was two-years-old.

The greatest desire in my world of dreams was to be a missionary to Africa. While praying in an empty church at the early age of ten, God spoke clearly to my heart that I would be a missionary to Africa. I remember the time, now more than 55 years ago, like it was just yesterday. With tears streaming down my face in worship to the Lord that I loved more than life, I said, "Lord, if You really have called me to Africa, tell me in no uncertain terms." I heard the Lord speak to my heart, "Turn around." I obeyed, and there lying on the pew behind me was a small typed piece of paper that said, "I have called you to Africa."

I knew from that moment on that no matter what came my way, I would one day end up on African soil. Young and impressionable with an imagination as big as the continent, I fantasized and I dreamed my dreams. I would grow up, leave home and family, live in a grass hut, die of the fever, and God would say "Well done," . . . or some such similar scenario. And as they say, whoever *they* are, "And that would be that."

With parents who encouraged me in ministry even though I was a girl, I felt as though I could do anything God asked of me. My school writings, plans, and dreams were consumed with thoughts of Africa.

As a child, God placed in my life wonderful people of great influence. William Caldwell, a missionary evangelist, was one of those heroes. In the early 1970s, I had the distinct privilege of ministering with him and his wife in Bombay, India to crowds of over 20,000 per night. My life was beginning to be ruined for the ordinary.

Missionary Evangelist Morris Plotts, known in Africa as "Bwana Tembo," was another of my champions of the Faith. While never losing the call God had placed in my heart for Africa at a young age, I worked for ten years taking evangelistic teams and planting churches in Mexico. On one very important day, Morris Plotts came to my husband's pastoral office at our church in Covington, Louisiana to ask him if I could go to Africa and head up a church planting team. Mike, who is my biggest hero of all and greatest blessing for a soul mate, said, "You don't even need to ask her. I know the answer is 'yes,' and I give my complete blessing. This will be a dream come true for Marigold."

In 1982, when I landed at Jomo Kenyatta Airport in Nairobi, Kenya, the call from God that had come to me so clearly in 1957 began to unfold. Although this was my first time to visit Kenya, tears of joy flowed freely, and I knew in my spirit that I was home.

As a young teen, another couple entered the playing field of influence in my future. They were Glenn and Marilyn Ford, missionaries to Kenya, Tanzania, and Ethiopia. Especially since I had admired them for so long, it was an honor for Mike and me to work in Tanzania, as well as Kenya, in crusade ministry with these two like-minded colleagues and true work fellows in the enterprise of winning souls. They knew how to organize a successful crusade, which I might add, is a lost art today. After spending a little time with Marilyn on a missions compound, I tried to imagine myself living the same. However, it never came to be, for God had a different plan for us which did not include that particular venue of ministry life. Mike and I were to be evangelists in every sense of the word. We live wherever duty calls, with tents as our home and vehicles to take us to the unreached, untaught masses of humanity.

I have tried for years to divide my time between adventures in Africa and numerous other countries. In spite of hardships—including malaria, typhoid, even a rabid monkey bite (with rabies series to follow); being chased by elephants (quite frightening) and stalked by lions; hundreds of flats and vehicle breakdowns; nasty river water baths; ground holes and bush latrines;

tents for homes with multiplied backaches from sleeping on the ground; and a myriad of hostile dudu ("bugs") that all seemed to have radar to find me no matter how hard I tried to hide from them—still I am overwhelmed with gratitude and thankfulness that God called me, and not someone else, from the predictable world of the ordinary to a life of insane adventure to follow His call and my dreams. I love the work like a sixteen-year-old schoolgirl! Each new dawn breaks forth with challenges and victories offering no two days alike. I'm actually writing this from a tent erected in the bush lands of Kenya between outreach efforts.

You will find in this volume and others to follow a mixture of fun, adventure, hardships, tears, mayhem, rescues, and victories. The stories in the *Chronicles of the Call* series tell of lives completely dependent on the grace and mercy of God to provide constant protection and provision against all odds. I will relate the stories of our son's terrible burn that nearly cost him his life, our daughter's deliverance from the power of the destroyer, travels across 83 countries as missionary evangelists, victories over cancer, and tales from our personal anecdotes while living a nomadic existence on the Dark Continent of Africa for the purpose of spreading the gospel.

Some of the stories are hard to believe, but they are completely true with no embellishment. We have lived through the horror to tell the tales so that God might be glorified in all we say and do, and that you, the reader, may be encouraged to believe for the impossible in your life. I have personally seen God instantly heal the deaf, crippled, mute, raise the dead, and close the mouth of the lion. I have felt His great hand of deliverance in my personal life. I have also sat beside His saints—the young and the old that He has promoted to that great cloud of witnesses in glory. Yes, the only way to describe it is: *"Ruined for the Ordinary."*

1
MAN-EATERS OF LEKANKA

Night of the Lions

1

MAN-EATERS OF LEKANKA

Night of the Lions

No one ever imagines himself eyed by a stealth killer, licking his lips and dreaming of sinking his long white canines into tender flesh, providing his next meal, thus becoming prey for the predator. Nevertheless, when you make your home in tents in the bush lands of Kenya, you must be ready for anything, including the prospect of a man-eating lion dropping by for a late-night snack. Sounds unbelievable, but it happened.

Just a few miles from where we were camping only one year before, the niece of Moses Sayo, the General Superintendent for the Assemblies of God Maasai Mara District, was fetching water from a nearby small water hole for her three little children. The lions were lying in wait for her. She was killed and devoured by the man-eaters. The lions were never killed, leaving them to continue their stalking of humans. They earned the name of "Man-eaters of Lekanka." Many times we encounter villagers who live with wounds and bear witness that they indeed miraculously survived such attacks. These incidents make us keenly aware that the man-eaters of Lekanka roam the area where we were camping.

There were twelve of us camping in the Loita Plains grasslands. We had two teams working with us from the States—a medical team and a children's ministry team. Dr. Adam White, our son-in-law, headed up the medical aspects of the mission; and Melissa White, our daughter and a children's pastor in the States, led the children's ministry team. We were targeting villages within driving distance that we knew had not been reached with the gospel. God was greatly blessing the efforts. In the evenings we came in exhausted, but with a feeling of accomplishment.

We had seven tents set up in a semi-circle with a large fire in the middle near a seasonal river that was dry for the most part during this time of the year. On either side of the river stood very old large acacia umbrella trees and a thicket of smaller thorn trees, bushes, and dense underbrush, giving a jungle effect then dwindling into the wide open savannah. About 50 yards away, we had a few more tents with another fire where the translators and cook slept and prepared food. Just beyond the food area, we parked the vans, land cruiser, and truck. We also hired guards to keep the fires going throughout the night and walk the perimeter to protect us from the potential dangers of elephants, lions, leopards, hyenas, wild dogs, and other predatory animals. Mike always ensured plenty of firewood was gathered from trees that had been destroyed by elephants during the night. Why they love to uproot trees, killing them, I'll never understand.

The night started like any other when camping in the bush of Africa. I usually prefer to be the last one to bathe so I can go straight away to my tent to avoid the night mosquitoes. If people are sitting around the fire, I feel I should be there to keep them company. Besides, I don't want to miss anything. Eating popcorn—the one luxury that my husband insists on—while sitting around the fire on a star-filled night is enjoyable.

With night approaching, the exhilarating red sun setting quickly, the camp began to settle down to what seemed to be a restful evening. Taking a pail, I took a couple of quarts of hot water out of the large pot sitting on top of the fire, added about as much cool water, and carried it to a little makeshift shower placed neatly under the trees.

The shower was one of Cabala's finest, made of nylon, a 4X4 cubicle with netting on top to allow viewing the sun, moon, or stars, whatever the case may be, while washing away the dirt and cares of the day. The floor was lined with plastic to keep one from standing in the mud during showers. All the newcomers to camp life are shown just how easy it can be to cleanse the body as well as wash your hair with less than a gallon of water. I call it the dip, level, and pour method. You simply dip your cup into the warmed water and pour it over your body, starting at the top of your head. By the time you have lathered up and rinsed off, you are squeaky clean. I'm sure it was done this way in the Wild West. It's not like soaking one's tired body in a warm Jacuzzi, but it gets the job done.

When I exited the shower, the beautiful sunset was long gone, and dusk was spreading its dark wings over the camp; so I hurried back to the safety of my tent, and prepared to crawl into my sleeping bag lying on top of the air mattress. I did something that night I have not done before or since. The crackling fire's glow casting eerie spidery shadows writhing and twisting on the Bass Pro nylon tent walls greatly disturbed my ability to drift into blissful sleep. I took some neat sheets—a waterproof lightweight floor cover often found in lawn or pet departments that is the size of a flat sheet. It makes a great carpet for the tent floor due to the fact that it keeps the damp cold earth from seeping through and chilling one's bones. The cloth also blocks light, so I pinned them to the walls of our tent using clothespins, immediately throwing it into blackness. This made for much better sleeping. With the help of my faithful flashlight, I inspected my sleeping bag one more time for any unwanted guest that might have crawled in. I wiggled down into the bag, zipped it tightly, placed my sweet little light under my pillow, and immediately entered into a deep sleep.

Floating, floating on a cloud in heaven, light as a feather I swayed. With not a care or pain, I floated. Then I fell off the cloud and began to float, float, float back to earth. With a thud I hit the ground, flipping my air mattress over on top of me. I had been dreaming. I was zipped so tightly and tangled in my sleeping bag and other covers with the mattress on top of me, that I had no choice but to wake Mike to be rescued from my calamity.

The night was frigid and the last thing he wanted to do was to crawl out of his warm sleeping bag, but of course he did; always my hero, my knight in shining armor. However, he mumbled quite a few complaints about the extra blankets over my sleeping bag, saying these were the reason I had flipped my mattress. I am surprised we didn't wake the whole camp with the noise we made. When my mattress flipped, it hit the canvas nightstand holding my extra batteries, water, vitamins, and everything I wanted to keep off the damp floor, and sent things flying in all directions with much clanging. Stumbling around in the dark locating flashlights and remaking my little bed, we made even more banging noises.

When I finally lay back down, it was 1:32 a.m. I said, "God why did You let me fall out of my bed? You know how badly I need my sleep." The voice I have come to know as my Lord's clearly said to me, "I woke you up on purpose."

As I tried to discern why God saw it necessary to wake me up at this early hour, I heard the faint noises whispering outside of my tent like wraiths in the night. Something was not right.

With all senses on alert, I lay there listening. My mind began to reflect back to a night when we were staying in tents in Tanzania's Tarengire Game Park. Gary and Linda Ankrom, Bob and Ruby Hoke, and Mike and I were traveling in Tanzania in crusade ministry, and decided to overnight in a quaint, modest tented camp. The canvas tents lined the top ridge of a not-so-large escarpment. There were no fences, and the small tents were rather far apart. Mike and I, for some unknown reason, had moved our little cots together into the middle of the floor of our tent, leaving about a foot of space between our tent beds and the canvas walls. We unzipped the windows and settled down to enjoy an evening of wilderness bliss. On a little mound of dirt right beside our tent stood the world's smallest antelope, a dik-dik. Far in the distance, we could hear lions roaring back and forth calling to each other. Because music is such a prominent part of my life, it gives me a tiny edge on sound movements and distance.

"Mike, it sounds like those lions are coming this way. They sound closer than a few minutes ago." I said as we tucked into bed.

"As long as that little dik-dik is standing here and not running, we have nothing to worry about," Mike said.

Naturally, we had chosen the very last tent to stay in, partly for the seclusion, and partly for the fact that the only sounds we would hear were truly all animal. I looked at my watch when the lions began roaring; it read 9:00 p.m. The generator would be turned off around 10:00 p.m., leaving us with only a flashlight—or torch as the Africans call it. I continued listening to the lions and watching the dik-dik. The generator shut down, and the entire camp was thrown into blackness. I tried to fall asleep, awareness growing deep in my spirit of something amiss. I tossed and turned in a fitful effort to sleep. The lions became silent. The only thing that makes me more anxious than a huffing, growling lion in the night is one that becomes silent, making it difficult to know its location. I did not notice when the dik-dik ran for cover.

At precisely 2:00 am, in the darkness, a sudden noise made my nerves flair. The silence was abruptly broken with lion commotion. Air seeped from my throat as roaring, snarling, growling lions mated three feet from my head outside our unzipped windows. We were separated from the obscene big cats with only mesh netting walls. I slipped my hand under Mike's covers to squeeze his hand.

He whispered, "Don't move; don't breathe."

We lay there perfectly still for seemingly an eternity, our hands in a tight grip under the cover, praying that the lions would take their amorous activities elsewhere. Their violent, furious roars during mating must scare them, because they certainly do scare me! We thought they would never leave.

Eventually they roamed off, making their sinister growls and roaring, walking right by the Hokes' and then Ankroms' tents. As Mike heard the padding of their paws fading in the distance he stealthily, as not to draw attention, slipped out of bed and simply hooked the window flaps rather than zipping them shut. The zipper would have made a huge sound in the still night, and it could have turned them back on us.

When it comes to lions, two of the most dangerous situations you can find yourself confronted with are mating lions, and lionesses with cubs. As sunlight broke over the horizon, Mike went outside to measure the large male footprints, curious to see just how close they were to us. The paw tracks were three feet from the tent wall parallel with my head. Ouch!! No wonder my body quivered at their frightful sounds!

When we saw the guards the next morning, we asked them where they were during the night when we needed them. They replied, "Hiding in the tool shed. You know the lions were in the camp!" We all gave a chuckle, but did agree that those guards did not deserve their pay for the night.

Because the sounds outside my tent now were so much different than in the Tarengire, I entertained the thought that maybe we had two-legged animals rather than the four-legged type ghosting through the blackness of the night. *"What about the guard outside of our tent? Surely he was aware of the presence of a sinister guest,"* I thought.

Because of the neat sheets I had hung earlier, I could not see the fire. However, there was no crackling sound of fire, only the rough breathing of a heavy animal on the other side of the nylon wall that sent chill bumps dancing up and down my spine like line dancers at a country hoedown.

"Lions!" The voice whispered to my heart— *"Lions!"* I lay perfectly still with my eyes wide—all senses on full alert, straining to hear anything to disprove what I felt the Lord had just revealed to me. I listened—straining to hear more intensely as the vague, stealthy, secretive sounds continued wafting into our tent. There was no doubt in my mind that lions were just outside. The night seemed to tremble, and my heart tripped over itself. Mike, being so tired, had already drifted back into the rhythmic breathing of a light snore. Under ordinary conditions his light, steady breathing would be comforting. But not tonight! Not now!

My mouth opened to scream *"Lions!"* Only a whisper escaped.

"Mike, wake up! There are lions outside our tent." Even though my mouth moved, no sound came out.

Ever so slowly I sat up, my heart skittering from the adrenalin. *Whoosh, whoosh*, I could hear my blood pumping in my head. For a moment, the lions hesitated. With heightened senses, I strained to hear. Then another noise—a soft thump on the dirt outside as large thick pads tried to slip silently through the night! Heavy breathing!

I stopped breathing altogether.

"Mike, wake up!" Still I could not make a sound! My mind's eyes imagined the massive predators sniffing the air, smelling my fear. *"Oh God, help us! Let it not be lions!"* But I knew it was!

Knowing in my heart that God had awakened me on purpose, quite possibly to save our lives, I tried to silently speak, so as not to provoke the beast to a full blown attack on us, "Mike!" Slightly louder than a whisper, "Mike wake up; we have . . ." (ROAR) ". . . Lions!"

A male lion interrupted my statement with a charge roar that seemingly lasted for an eternity— a solid vortex of unbelievable sounds that drowned out everything else.

It is said that a lion's roar can be heard for over five miles, and a charging lion covers 100 yards in three seconds.

Time leapt into a nightmare dance. My mouth sagged open! My breath caught in my throat! My heart stopped beating! Snatching a breath and scrambling for my heart to balance itself again after the skipped beats, I shook like a leaf trembling in the wind, with every nerve tingling.

Four hard amber eyes glared hungrily across our camp as they were deciding a new plan of attack.

Now I shakily stepped to my window and screamed, "Everyone get out of bed, but don't leave your tent! There are lions in the camp!" There was no guard in sight! The fire was out!

Due to all the noise, the lions froze in place for a moment in a shadowy skeleton of thorn bushes and fallen trees.

Our guard, Kantai Ole Ndoinyo (we called him *Jackson*) stretched and calmly walked toward the cook area to get a cup of chai, a mixture of tea, milk, and sugar—still unaware of a healthy male lion in the prime of life, accompanied by a hungry irate female skulking in the shadows. As he reached for the teapot, the lion roared from near our tent, the area he had just left. He was instantly aware of his imminent danger. Later I learned that when I fell out of bed, the commotion had awakened the sleeping guard next to our tent who was unaware of crouching death only feet away.

In my peripheral vision I saw Mike unzipping our tent. He wore no shirt, no shoes, just his pants as he stepped out into the jaws of the inky blackness of the African night.

"Where are you going?" I asked, my voice laced with palatable fear.

"To fight the lions," Mike said.

"Zip the tent," I replied.

Later I asked Mike if he wasn't afraid when he had to walk right into the midst of the lions, unable to see where they were. His reply, "I didn't think about it. It just had to be done to protect everyone." More than just a little spooked, it whispered a tale of horror to what could have been, had it not been for the protection of the Lion of the tribe of Judah, the King of kings, and the Lord of lords.

To say that God had sent angels to protect would be an understatement. By all natural rights, as he bravely walked with purpose, showing no fear, right by the lions to reach our vehicle some fifty yards away, Mike should have been killed. The old white land cruiser, which we call the *Simba,* never started without being pushed. However, on this dreadful night, the old darling started with the first turn of the key as if to say, *"We're in this together."*

Mike turned the bright lights of the land cruiser right into the amber eyes of the now confused lions. He began to chase them out of camp—a healthy strong male lion and a strong female lioness. Determined to have us for dinner, the lions circled down into the dry riverbed approximately a half mile away, and came right back to camp. Mike continued to follow their every move with the spotlights of the four-wheel drive cruiser.

After chasing them out of our camp the second time, Mike had his own battle between himself and the determined lions. A sinister rumble rose in the air! The nearly 10-foot, 500-pound, healthy male lion crouched behind a thorn bush, waiting for another chance to enter camp to continue his hunt. His two-inch claws gripped the earth, ready to take purchase if need be. Mike never broke his speed as the land cruiser bounced over hyena holes in the savannah. The old boy thought the thorn bush hid him, but Mike continued quickly toward him. Mike didn't really want to hit him, but wanted the lions to know they were not welcome in our camp. When the lovebird lions concluded that they weren't going to be successful in their pursuit of a snack at our expense, they gave up the fight and retreated in the opposite direction of the camp.

While Mike's battle was ensuing out on the plains, I peered out of my window, still trembling, and noticed Jeff, one of the team members, standing in the doorway of his tent. I shouted, "What are you doing? Stay inside!" With much stuttering, he exclaimed that when the lion gave his ear-blasting roar splicing the night, he had been sitting up, trying to decide if it was safe for him to go out to relieve himself. Very thankfully, he had not done so.

Moses Sayo, Jeff's tent mate, had been startled out of a deep sleep at the earth-shattering roar of the lion. He shook so hard he couldn't unzip the zipper on the tent. So in light of everything, he ripped open the zipper as Jeff was trying to hold the zipper together!

Those of us at camp knew that we had to stoke the fire to build it up for protection. Rick and

Bonna's tent was very near the glowing embers. Rick asked, "Do you want me to stoke the fire?"

"Please, you're the nearest tent to the fire." I said.

Rick, an ex-Marine, stepped out into the dark night for more wood to add to the fire. When the fire began to blaze once again, we all joined one another around the safety of the flames.

Melissa, our daughter, tried to wake her sleeping husband, Adam, who had managed to sleep through the whole ordeal. He simply said, "Go back to sleep; it's probably just an elephant." Had it been *just an elephant*, we still could have been in serious trouble, for in some ways, they are more dangerous than lions. They tend to charge tents and kill people just because they can.

When Jeff joined us around the fire, he said, "I have a word of prophecy. I will not sleep tonight. I will not sleep tomorrow night. I will not sleep until I get back on the plane headed to America."

Although the noise had frightened the ambient sounds of the insects into anxious silence, soon their rhythmic, harmonious sounds began coaxing all of us back toward slumber with their peaceful night songs.

While writing this story, I met a Dr. Sankok due to an unwanted set of circumstances, and picked up more information concerning these man-eaters. I thought to give his words a place in my notes so the readers have a better knowledge of just how dangerous the situation was with the Lekanka lions on that fateful night.

Our grandson Michael, twin to Maurice, came down with heavy shakes and a scalding fever while he was visiting us in Kenya and taking part in ministry. He was playing the guitar and ministering at a children's outreach in Narok. When I placed my hand on his knees, I could feel the joints trembling; we immediately were concerned that he might have malaria. I recognized many of the symptoms, having had the dreaded sickness more times than I care to recall.

Having heard about him, Dr. Sankok drove up at our camp while we were packing to take Michael to the hospital in Nairobi. Although he is a surgeon in a Nairobi hospital, Dr. Sankok runs a tropical disease clinic in Narok. We had never met the man, but he knew of us through Moses.

Through a series of lab tests, Dr. Sankok confirmed that Michael indeed had malaria and started treatment immediately. In the course of making small talk to help pass the time for Michael while the quinine was administered, I told Dr. Sankok about my writings concerning the night of the lions. The truth about lions was the last thing I had on my mind at this moment in time. I would rather stare down lions than to watch my grandson fighting malaria; however, Michael enjoyed listening to the stories.

He said, "I know those lions well. I have treated many wounded people after they narrowly escaped an encounter with them, and know of at least nine souls they have killed. It is a miracle you escaped. You were blessed and protected by God to have not been killed by those beasts."

The bushes and thorn brush on the back sides of our tents should have discouraged predators from coming in too close. However, I have heard of lions jumping these barricades, landing right in the middle of a Maasai boma, and killing whatever got in their path of destruction. I talked with a family in Siana Springs, an area just down the road from our camp, who lost their child to a lion just that way. The lion jumped the fence, landing on top of their house—crushing in the mud structure—and once inside, snatched their child and leaped out and away, escaping with its late night snack.

When lions develop a taste for humans, they will feed on man to the exclusion of other prey. One thing is certain, if a lion is hungry enough and you are there, man-eater or not, he will eat you. To this day these beasts still roam in the area of our Bible school and camp.

All things happen for a reason, I believe, and the experience with the *Man-eaters of Lekanka* is no exception. That night standing around the protection of the fire, God birthed a message in my heart. It is like a fire shut up in my bones: Don't let the fire go out, or you become PREY FOR THE PREDATOR.

2
PREY FOR THE PREDATOR

Don't Let the Fire Go Out!

2

PREY FOR THE PREDATOR

Don't Let the Fire Go Out!

"When you allow the fire for God—that once burned hot within you—to grow cold, then you become prey for the predator of your soul. The Bible tells us that Satan goes about like a roaring lion, roaming to and fro, seeking whomever he may devour. We know that our adversary, the devil, does not play fair. He kicks you when you're down. He lies to you when you are discouraged. He cannot tell the truth. The Bible says that he was a liar from the beginning, and the truth is not in him. Lying is his native tongue.

A hot fire will keep lions and other predators from attacking you in the night. The fire of God, burning brightly within you, will keep away the predator of your soul. Satan has to flee the presence of God!

In both the Old and New Testaments, fire is associated with the divine presence of God. So let's look at the Scriptures. Let's see how important it is to keep the fire burning on the altar of our hearts.

Don't let the fire go out!

Leviticus 6:12-13 NASU,
The fire on the altar shall be kept burning on it. It shall not go out, but the priest shall burn wood on it every morning; and he shall lay out the burnt offering on it, and offer up in smoke the fat portions of the peace offerings on it. Fire shall be kept burning continually on the altar; it is not to go out.

It is important that we keep the fire of the Lord burning deep inside us. Our love for Him is like a fire. His Spirit is alive within us.

I would like to point out just a few Biblical illustrations where God revealed Himself to man. In these accounts, YOU WILL FIND FIRE PRESENT.

1. **You will find FIRE present in the making of God's covenant with Abraham.**

    Genesis 15:17-18 NASU,
    It came about when the sun had set, that it was very dark, and behold, there appeared a smoking oven and a flaming torch which passed between these pieces. On that day the Lord made a covenant with Abram, saying, "To your descendants I have given this land, from the river of Egypt as far as the great river, the river Euphrates."

2. **You will find FIRE present in the burning bush with Moses.**

    Exodus 3:2-4 NASU,
    The angel of the LORD appeared to him in a blazing fire from the midst of a bush; and he looked, and behold, the bush was burning with fire, yet the bush was not consumed.

    So Moses said, "I must turn aside now and see this marvelous sight, why the bush is not burned up."

When the LORD saw that he turned aside to look, God called to him from the midst of the bush and said, "Moses, Moses!" And he said, "Here I am."

Then He said, "Do not come near here; remove your sandals from your feet, for the place on which you are standing is holy ground."

3. You will find FIRE present in the pillar of fire.

The children of Israel were led out of slavery and bondage by night. God led them out by a pillar of fire.

Exodus 13:21-22 NASU,
The Lord was going before them in a pillar of cloud by day to lead them on the way, and in a pillar of fire by night to give them light, that they might travel by day and by night. He did not take away the pillar of cloud by day, nor the pillar of fire by night, from before the people.

4. You will find FIRE present on Sinai.

Exodus 19:18-19 NASU,
Now Mount Sinai was all in smoke because the Lord descended upon it in fire; and its smoke ascended like the smoke of a furnace, and the whole mountain quaked violently. When the sound of the trumpet grew louder and louder, Moses spoke and God answered him with thunder.

5. **You will find FIRE in the flame on the altar.**

Judges 13:20 NASU,
For it came about when the flame went up from the altar toward heaven, that the angel of the Lord ascended in the flame of the altar. When Manoah and his wife saw this, they fell on their faces to the ground.

6. **You will find that FIRE came from heaven when Solomon's Temple was consecrated.**

2 Chronicles 7:1-3 NKJV,
When Solomon had finished praying, fire came down from heaven and consumed the burnt offering and the sacrifices; and the glory of the LORD filled the temple. And the priests could not enter the house of the

LORD, because the glory of the LORD had filled the LORD's house. When all the children of Israel saw how the fire came down, and the glory of the LORD on the temple, they bowed their faces to the ground on the pavement, and worshiped and praised the LORD, saying: "For He is good, For His mercy endures forever."

7. **You will find that FIRE was present when revealing that our God is the true and the living God—"The God that Answered by Fire"—Yahweh.**

1 Kings 18:24 NASU,
"Then you call on the name of your god, and I will call on the name of the Lord, and the God who answers by fire, He is God." And all the people said, "That is a good idea."

1 Kings 18:28-29 NASU,
So they cried with a loud voice and cut themselves according to their custom with swords and lances until the blood gushed out on them. When midday was past, they raved until the time of the offering of the evening sacrifice; but there was no voice, no one answered, and no one paid attention.

1 Kings 18:37-38 NASU,
"Answer me, O Lord, answer me, that this people may know that You, O Lord, are God, and that You have turned their heart back again." Then the fire of the Lord fell and consumed the burnt offering and the wood and the stones and the dust, and licked up the water that was in the trench.

Fire Purging Iniquities

We find yet another powerful message in the story of Isaiah's vision.

First, it is an upward vision. Then the vision turns inwardly. Lastly, the vision turns outwardly to a lost world.

A Vision That Is:
Upward . . .
Inward . . .
Outward

The touch of the fire of God begins as we focus upward upon Him. This is the key factor. He touches our heart, spirit, and mind with His fire from His altar. Then after He has taken our iniquities from us (inwardly cleansing us), He asks that we be His representatives.

This is one of my most favorite illustrations regarding the personal presence of our dear Lord in our lives; His cleansing power—transforming power—the call from His heart to our souls to reach the lost.

> Isaiah 6:6-7 KJV,
> *Then flew one of the seraphims unto me, having a live coal in his hand, which he had taken with the tongs from off the altar: And he laid it upon my mouth, and said, Lo, this hath touched thy lips; and thine iniquity is taken away, and thy sin purged.*

I particularly love this passage, because the fire of God touches our mouth. The power of life and death is in the tongue. If the fire of God has touched us, we will certainly love those of the household of God. Even the wicked love those that love them. However, we, who have been touched by the power of God, will love our enemies—those who lie about us, those who use us for their personal gain, those who would kill us if they could. We will love them, do good to them, and pray for them.

We cannot do this on our own. It takes the fire of God burning away our selfishness and fault-finding spirit; His fire touching our lips, purging our iniquities.

After He has touched us with fire from off His altar, He asks us to go for him. Our focus then turns outward to a needy world.

Yet another story of the saga of our lives tells the importance of unconditional forgiveness. God required unconditional forgiveness of me when a great injustice befell my family. Only after a visitation by God, I was willing to let go of the anger and to forgive, even though no forgiveness had been sought by the perpetrator.

I want to repeat these Scriptures. I often find myself praying that God will take a hot coal from off His altar and touch my lips so that I might speak His power, touch my heart so that I might feel His heart, and touch the ears of those who are listening, so that they will hear what His Spirit would say to them. I pray that people be changed, not just stirred.

> Isaiah 6:6-7 KJV,
> *Then flew one of the seraphims unto me, having a live coal in his hand, which he had taken with the tongs from off the altar: And he laid it upon my mouth, and said, Lo, this hath touched thy lips; and thine iniquity is taken away, and thy sin purged.*

Now turn your focus to verse 8:

I heard the voice of the Lord, saying, Whom shall I send, and who will go for us? Then said I, Here am I; send me.

God is not willing that any would perish. When man has been freshly touched by divine fire, God asks, "Who will go for us?"

When our hearts and souls have been touched with the fire of God, we realize what sinners we are. But, God has removed that sin from us! How can we deny His one request, "WHO WILL GO FOR US?"

At that moment, we are able to say, "HERE AM I, LORD, SEND ME."

God knows the sinfulness of carnal flesh, our tendency for selfishness. To represent God means living a selfless life, often without the simple pleasures of life. It means keeping silent when man has pushed all your buttons. It means turning the other cheek, so to speak. We cannot do these things in our own self. They require a touch from the fire of God.

Even if man could earn a merit and live a sacrificial life by his own choice, he certainly could not purge his own sins and iniquities. It takes a divine encounter with God. There are no grandchildren born into salvation. This is a one-on-one experience with a divine, powerful God of fire. This is a moment . . . time . . . experience . . . vision one will forever remember.

> Isaiah 6:9 KJV,
> *And he said, Go, and tell this people, Hear ye indeed, but understand not; and see ye indeed, but perceive not.*

Let's view a few more statements the Bible says about **FIRE.**

He will make His **MINISTERS A FLAMING FIRE.**

> Psalm 104:4 KJV,
> *Who makes his angels spirits; his ministers a flaming fire.*

The Word of God was like **FIRE SHUT UP IN MY BONES.**

> Jeremiah 20:9 KJV,
> *Then I said, I will not make mention of him, nor speak any more in his name. But his word was in mine heart as a burning fire shut up in my bones, and I was weary with forbearing, and I could not stay.*

This should make us hunger for the Word of God, and for His Spirit. It should make us eager to read His Word and hide it in our hearts. For it is like a "fire shut up in my bones," screaming to be shared, searching for release, shouting to be lived.

The **FIRE** is birthed within us through the Word.

The Word of God is sharper than any two-edged sword, cutting and dividing the body, soul, and spirit.

FIRE OF THE HOLY GHOST

He will baptize you with the Holy Ghost and **FIRE.**

> Matthew 3:11 KJV,
> *I indeed baptize you with water unto repentance: but he that cometh after me is mightier than I, whose shoes I am not worthy to bear: he shall baptize you with the Holy Ghost, and with fire.*

The Holy Ghost is the very Spirit of God. You say, "What Spirit?" He is that same Spirit who raised Christ from the dead. He dwells in you. That same Spirit will quicken your mortal body!

FIRE is still associated with the presence of God, even in the New Testament. God has not changed, nor ever will change.

52

Luke 3:16 KJV,
John answered, saying unto them all, I indeed baptize you with water; but one mightier than I cometh, the latchet of whose shoes I am not worthy to unloose: he shall baptize you with the Holy Ghost and with fire:

If the Old Testament and New Testament saints needed the fire of God, then so do we. We should seek God's presence; not fight it. We need to be baptized with the Holy Ghost of God and His fire. We need a divine encounter with the Holy One of Israel—Yahweh—the God who answers by fire.

We wonder why many fall prey to the predator? If you look at my story of the night of the lions, it was because the fire—which was to protect us— had gone out. Therefore, I personally believe the answer is found in these passages. We shake our heads when Christians cut each other down, and churches split once again. We marvel when a great warrior of the faith falls into a trap cunningly set to destroy him.

It boils down to this: Have you been purged by the fire of God? We are just humans, and we must each be personally and individually touched by the fire of God. Our minds must be renewed.

God is Spirit, and we must worship Him in spirit and truth. We must be filled with His Spirit. The carnal mind cannot receive the things of God.

Let's look at just one more passage that encourages us to be Spirit-led children of God.

But God has revealed them to us through His Spirit (verse 10).

> 1 Corinthians 2:9-16 NKJV,
> *But as it is written: "Eye has not seen, nor ear heard, Nor have entered into the heart of man the things which God has prepared for those who love Him."* **But God has revealed them to us through His Spirit.** *For the Spirit searches all things, yes, the deep things of God. For what man knows the things of a man except the spirit of the man which is in him? Even so no one knows the things of God except the Spirit of God. Now we have received, not the spirit of the world, but the Spirit who is from God, that we might know the things that have been freely given to us by God. These things we also speak, not in words which man's wisdom teaches but which the Holy Spirit teaches, comparing spiritual things with spiritual. But the natural man does not receive the things of the Spirit of God, for they are*

foolishness to him; nor can he know them, because they are spiritually discerned. But he who is spiritual judges all things, yet he himself is rightly judged by no one. For "who has known the mind of the Lord that he may instruct Him?" But we have the mind of Christ.

Don't let the fire go out in your heart, or you become prey for the predator.

During that night, the lions came *"seeking to devour us."* We were unprotected—fair game—all because we had allowed the fire to grow cold. The keeper of the fire had fallen asleep. This almost cost us our lives.

My friend, never allow your fiery love for Jesus to grow cold, or you may find yourself prey for the predator of your soul—Satan himself.

KEEP THE FIRE BURNING!

3
A GOD THING

Meeting Moses

3

A GOD THING

Meeting Moses

I walked the streets of Narok, a Maasai town half-way between the escarpment and the game reserve, searching for an African man I had never met. How was I to find him? There must be 50,000 people walking in the streets, and my Swahili was only good enough to get me in trouble, but not good enough to get me out of trouble. There were sixteen people with me on this mission, mostly pastors and their wives. Mike had remained in the United States tending to the duties of pastoring.

That morning at the Utalii Hotel in Nairobi I had met with the acting field director, an American missionary who supervised all the activities and outreaches of his assigned territory. We had overnighted, readying ourselves for the trip to Masai land. This ministry outreach had been months in the making. It was before the time of cell phones in Kenya. The field director informed me of a man by the name of Moses Ole Sayo, a young single Maasai, who lived in Narok and spoke English quite well. He said that I could inquire around town and surely find him without too much trouble.

I asked, "Have you notified him that I am coming?"

He emphatically said, "No. There is no phone communication, and I have not been there to tell him. But you should have no problem finding him." Foolishly, I believed him.

After our meeting was over, we packed up and headed for Narok. Crossing the Great Rift Valley as we came off the escarpment indicated that our bus had officially left civilization for the more primitive roads ahead. Travel was slow. The roads were dirty and dusty. I had rented a 20-passenger bus for the two weeks of ministry. Following the mountains, the roads stretched out looking parched and barren. A few gazelle grazed on the plains. Once in a while, we would spot a giraffe, and excitement would ripple through the bus. What seemed like an eternity passed before we finally arrived in Narok. Due to the bad roads, it took much longer than I had anticipated. Upon arrival, I was amazed to realize it was not a small village where I could just walk up to people asking about this man, Moses. Rather, it was a large town, and I realized I might not find him at all.

I pulled to the side of the road and asked the team to pray with me for God to point me in the right direction. We joined hands and agreed together that God would quickly direct me to this man. I knew we only had a 45-minute window to connect with Moses. We had to arrive before 6:00 pm at the gate to the Mara game reserve, where we had found the only lodging for the ministry that we were involved in; and we were yet a four-hour drive, excluding problems, from the entrance.

Asking the dedicated group to continue praying, I exited the bus and I walked the streets in search of Moses. I walked alone, not wanting to put any of the jet-lagged team in harm's way. I didn't know this town or its residents, but I felt no fear. I walked about two miles. I made my way down paths that had holes as deep as I am tall. Trash laid everywhere. The smells of garbage, human waste, and cow dung assaulted my senses. People cooked out on the dust-laden streets with *jikos* —a small eight-to-ten-inch in diameter cast iron charcoal grill that sits on the ground. I continued my stroll down the streets of the unfamiliar town, praying, "Oh, God, please help me to locate this man, *haraka*." (Swahili for *rapidly.*) People, walking who knows where, surrounded me on both sides. I just kept walking and praying. In front of a hotel called Spurs which was on the other side of the road, I saw two men walking side-by-side. Only a child of God will understand what I am about to say. These two men looked *saved*. My heart leaped within my chest. I felt compelled toward them. Avoiding the cattle in the middle of the road, I wound my way through the animals and people, and approached the men.

I ask, "Are you Moses Ole Sayo?"

"Yes, I am," he replied.

"Oh, praise God! Can you join us in Maasai land, and translate for me and my team of ministers?"

With a smile on his face, he said, "I am ready. Can Simon come as well?" Simon was the man walking with him.

"Yes, of course, he is more than welcome. We must hurry, though, or we will not make the gate before it closes for the night."

Much to my surprise as we walked the two-mile trek back to the bus, he reached behind a wall and grabbed a briefcase. With bags in hand, both Moses and Simon boarded the bus that would take us to the beginnings of a lifelong ministry together to the Maasai. Today, Moses is like a son to Mike and me.

I dared not talk on the bus in the open gritty ai,r or I would lose my voice, so I sat in silence until we finally reached our destination at "dark thirty." I rushed to get the team into their rooms. The place had no fences, and there were lions and elephants all around. The most important thing seemed to get everyone settled before the dark African night engulfed us.

Moses finally said to me, "Mama, can you sit down for a minute and let us tell you what happened?" I really wanted to get my luggage to my own room, but felt that what he had to say was very important.

"Oh, Moses, forgive me, I have been so absorbed with my team that I have not even properly introduced myself to you. My name is Marigold Cheshier. I thank you so much for being willing to come with us to preach the Word to the Maasai."

I ordered tea with milk and sugar for the three of us, and settled back to hear what this stranger had to say. There were vervet monkeys playing all around as we tried to converse. Hearing a hippo in the distance snorting, I wondered how close it was to us.

"Mama, no one told me you were coming. The gospel has not been preached to the Maasai of the Mara. Last night, God woke me, and spoke to me. He told me to pack my bags and be prepared to travel; that I was to interpret for someone coming to preach to the Maasai. Simon, my friend," pointing his hand to refer to his very small-of-stature companion, "had a similar experience. He lives in the Ngong Hills, far away from here. God spoke to him and told him the same thing. He started walking yesterday, and flagging matatus (vehicles that serve as taxis). He arrived this morning. We were walking and praying, asking God to reveal to us who He wanted us to work with. When we saw you walking down the street, I turned to Simon and said, 'That's who we're going to translate for; that woman coming. God is telling me that she is the one He wants us to interpret for.' Mama, this is a miracle, truly a miracle!"

I said, "Moses, yes, you are right. God has truly worked a miracle. This is a God thing."

4
SPOTTED TERROR

The Loita Hills Story

SPOTTED TERROR

The Loita Hills Story

It takes just one mistake, one night alone, one moment within the reach of the leopard's paw—and God, and God alone, to save you from certain death.

The Loita Hills are one of Kenya's last remaining true wilderness areas containing the most spectacular and unspoiled regions of Kenya, and rarely visited with a population of well over 200,000 traditional Maasai.

It wasn't just cold. It was a creeping, blood-congealing-in-the-veins cold. We settled down for a frigid night with the staccato chattering of my teeth sounding like a machine gun in the middle of a firefight. Uncontrolled shivering haunted my chilled bones. But even more troubling than my quivering body, were the eerie sounds wafting into my Boy Scout tent set up in the middle of the African plains. The distant yap of an occasional jackal, mingled with the hilarity of hyena laughs drifting in from the dark bush lands of Loita, made me question what other sinister creatures lurking in a fringe of dead grass and branches near our camp sought us out, plotting a deadly encounter. On this missionary journey, it would not be the lions that stalked us, but a huge—large-as-a-lioness—man-attacking male leopard.

A day earlier as the first blush of light burst out of hiding, we started our safari, leaving behind Nairobi's bustling city, the thick choking aroma of diesel, and our luggage that was "somewhere" (as the Africans are fond of saying) lost in flight. Soon we were passing tea and coffee fields and then the tall tree forest, just enjoying the cool of the morning. Suddenly without warning, we rounded a serpentine bend at the top of the escarpment with a breathtaking view of the Great Rift Valley below. Stunned by the sheer beauty of the escarpment and the land under the now bright sun, we pulled over to snap a quick photo.

Playing among the rocks were hyrax—rodent-like creatures a little bit like large squirrels. This proves that the Creator has an amazing sense of humor, as biologists tell us that these little

creatures are the nearest cousin to the elephant. The baboons, nature's hairy garbage disposals, strolled up and down the road, scavenging for food from passers-by. The whole scene looked like something that would appear in an art gallery. God, the great master Artist, capturedour minds with His creativity. We could see Mount Longonot, Hell's Gate, Mount Suswa, the Ngong Hills, and the Great Rift Valley stretched below us.

The East African Rift Valley is one the geologic wonders of the world. It's as if the creator took a giant sword and made a gaping wound in the surface of the earth approximately 6,000 kilometers (3,700 miles) in length from northern Syria in southwest Asia to central Mozambique in southeast Africa. The Rift Valley runs through Kenya clear to the Jordan River Valley.

The Great Rift Valley of Africa—formed by violent geological events of the past—is so prominent a cleft down the eastern side of the continent that it can be seen even from the moon. It is a spectacular sight to behold!

Our little caravan started the descent down the escarpment. This snake-like winding road with its hairpin curves that turn back on itself has a reputation as the most dangerous road in Kenya, with a natural rock wall on one side and a drop off into the valley on the other side. Over the years, we have seen many lorries—large trucks—that never made it around the curves, but ended up halfway down the mountain mangled by the protruding rocks and shrubs, most often with no survivors. Since there are no passing lanes for the entire trip down the mountain, I constantly watch for crazy drivers that impatiently pass slower vehicles. To pass a truck on this road is like playing Russian roulette with all the cylinders loaded. Whether I am the driver or passenger, each time we come off the mountain pass I let out a deep sigh of relief when arriving in Maai Mahiu at the base of this winding steep road.

Reaching Maai Mahiu, we turned west and proceeded across the dry and dusty rift valley floor with its occasional acacia thorn bushes sparsely freckling the landscape. Once we reached the other side of the valley, we started the long climb up the slopes to about 6000 feet above sea level. After reaching Narok, a small Maasai town, we headed toward the Loita plains. Hours of fighting dry dusty roads—even worse than a Louisiana logging road—had already begun to wear us down. Most of the time we preferred the ditch to the road due to the hundreds of pot holes in the so-called road. We then pointed the nose of the old green 1974 Land Rover—a real rattle trap—toward another set of mountains known as Loita Hills, our destination.

Forcing us to go off road—a term we use when the dirt roads play out and we follow only a trail—we continued our safari. The end goal was to present the good news of the saving power of Jesus Christ to a group of Maasai who had never seen white people or heard about Jesus.

As Mike is fond of saying, "No man should hear the gospel twice until all have heard it once."

Our mission trek occurred at the same time an article appeared in the *Mountain Movers* magazine, a media of the Assemblies of God. The sitting field director of East Africa stated that Loita Hills was one of the last un-penetrated areas in East Africa.

Night was quickly coming with scents from the bush lands wafting on the wind. We were already exhausted, windblown, wet with sweat, and nowhere near our destination.

Leaving the tarmac road, we began our arduous journey into the unknown of the Loita Hills. We had long left a normal road—normal being a definite matter of perspective—and were traveling by tracks made by obscure travelers before us. Now even this had disappeared into uncharted grasslands and volcanic rocks. We bounced from side to side as if on the world's bumpiest roller coaster.

"People pay good money in America for a ride like this," was my statement of consolation to any complaints. Though many theme parks have tried to duplicate such a safari, they have miserably failed.

We were crossing mountains and then valleys following no path, just the directions of our dear African friends. Since we had the only vehicle, whenever they came this deep into the bush, they walked. I must admit that even though the night sounds were captivating, it was intimidating to be slicing the night in a windowless vehicle across this harsh unknown land. I felt things could be lurking in the shadows of which one's worst nightmares consist. Yet there is an exhilarating excitement surrounding exploratory missions.

A little word about fear: Ninety-nine-percent of the things we fear never come to pass. The Word of God says, *"I have not given you the spirit of fear but of power, love and a sound mind."* Thoughts hung in my mind like a thick fog, and I grabbed on to them like a drowning swimmer reaching for a life buoy. "I am guarded by the King of kings, and the only thing to fear is fear itself. Angels are all around us, keeping guard over us."

The light of day was rapidly waning with the sky changing into brilliant orange and purple hues. We had known we would be setting up our tents after dark; that is, if we ever arrived somewhere to make camp. Personally, all I could think about was the slumbering bliss I hoped awaited all of us at the end of the trail.

Except for the occasional gazelle or zebra, there seemed to be nothing or no one around us as we cut through this large, open barren land. What we could not see through the covering of darkness were the many Maasai villages we were passing. Since they are made of cow manure and sticks and have no electricity, they completely blended with the dark of night.

 Finally, about 10:00 p.m. in the pitch dark, we arrived weary and worn out in the area where we were to begin ministry. "We are actually here," I told myself. I had begun to wonder if the place existed at all.

Excitement, mingled with trepidation, was flowing freely through my mind and heart like streams after a summer thunderstorm. Somewhere under the covering of darkness, we selected a spot to put up tiny tents and made camp in the Loita Hills, a place where the residents were totally unreached with the gospel.

What a privilege to be a voice for the Lord in this spiritually darkened and unreached land. A momentary shiver of raw fear rippled up my spine as I viewed the surrounding area under the blanket of night. A prayer escaped my lips in an inaudible whisper, "Lord, lead us to the place we can safely set up camp."

Three months before this eventful night, Mike, Mikey, and I had preached in Maasai villages on the eastern parts of the Maasai Mara of Kenya. We stayed at a tented camp called *Hippo*. Mikey, our son, was in a small canvas tent, while Mike and I were in a little round stone house with a grass roof. While that may seem to be a good thing, quite the contrary was actually true because the walls stopped a good foot before the roof began. This translates into no way to keep out snakes, rats, spiders, monkeys, or any creepy crawly creature that wanted to get into our space, while we were not looking, but mainly while we slept. I could envision some such creature sneaking within our covers. To ease my mind I carefully inspected the bed linens with a flashlight before slipping my feet beneath the covers—a routine I do till this day, and even then, I must still my imaginations of what might invade while we are in that nurturing state of sub-consciousness called sleep.

The cost of this faith building, mind-over-matter

experience was $35.00 per night per person, really more than we could afford. However, in the scheme of things, it's a small price to pay to reach people with the good news that Jesus saves. On Kenya's present economy, it is much worse, but still worth every penny. You can't put a price on a soul rescued from the pit of hell.

There is a place called the Sopa Lodge about a mile up the road near the top of a mountain. It's a place where rich people come from all over the world to have an African experience, which is the equivalent of watching the lions versus the Christians from the safety of a luxury box seat at the coliseum. We often walked there but could not even afford to buy a soda, much less stay the night, due to the fact that it was four times the cost of the Hippo Camp. However, it was good to stretch our legs from time to time, and the view from the lodge was spectacular. Had I known then what I know now, there would be no way I would walk such a distance with wild beasts lurking in the bushes that lined the paths we took. I'm convinced that my angels get overtime pay for their extra work in keeping me safe.

We preached in the villages just outside the park. We were at this location for a month, and then would move to another location for a month, endeavoring to minister to unreached people groups in the many villages located just outside of the game reserves.

While ministering in one of the nearby villages, a teacher from Loita Hills came to the saving knowledge of Jesus. He explained that in the Loita Hills there were thousands of people bound with witchcraft, and there were no churches of any kind. "Would you please come and bring this good news of Jesus to the people of Loita?" he asked.

After much prayer, we agreed to carry him back to his village and see for ourselves these thousands of people who had never heard about Jesus.

We left the Hippo Camp the next morning around 9:00 a.m. with this schoolteacher. We crossed rivers, sand beds, bush lands, and wound our way through dense forest, then over brown rolling hills of untamed and capricious high plateaus, and still could not reach the area. Although "give up" is not in our vocabulary, the bush's eerie shadows waved wildly with approaching darkness so we sadly had to concede and turn back.

Believing God had directed us, before daylight the following morning with a defiant determination we started the same journey—crossing the same rivers, sand beds, and plateaus—with joyful anticipation that we would triumph and reach our destiny.

After hours of sweltering heat, dust, and dirt covered bodies, we realized that once again we could not make it there and back in one day. One gift that God gave our family, if such a gift exists, is bulldog determination. The thing is, sometimes the jaw gets tired as your cramped muscles wane and you lose your grip. With the help of a supernatural God, who I might add, *will never ask you to do what He does not equip you to do*, we would accomplish this mission one way or another. Still holding on to the plan of accomplishing the goal, rationalizing our actions, we headed back to camp under a moonlit sky.

Ever etched in my memory would be this third morning. My spine tingled as we sliced through the still-lingering night and made our way along the same tracks we had followed the two previous days. Knowing that the famous Sand River with its dark, roiling, hazardous waters awaited us, and watching the bushland's shadowy paths swiping the sides of our old windowless Land Rover (which long since needed to be in a car graveyard), I silently whispered a prayer to God that He would allow no harm to come to us.

After two hours of traveling, the morning began to light up the skies like a chicken hatching from its warm egg. On one side we could see the moon, and on the other the rising sun. What a magnificent sight to behold! With much joy and a deep since of victory, we finally made it to the edge of the huge area called the Loita Hills. Even now, as I reflect on that moment, I can still feel the surge of the escalating emotions.

After ministering at this dear man's school, and learning of the enormous completely unreached region beyond, we gave our word that we would return. Our son, Mikey, was the first to say we needed to return with tents and spend whatever time and money needed to reach the lost in this faraway place.

Our return journey started with a lot of bantering dreams, visions, and excited anticipation of how we could keep our word and return to preach the gospel.

Thunderous clouds on the horizon demanded our attention. Soon our journey spun into a full-blown nightmare as the rain began with large menacing drops testing our resolve. A monsoon rained down upon us, bearing havoc in its wake. The old, slick-tired, 1974 Rover, rather than rolling, started sliding down the mountainside.

The dirt of this part of Kenya is made up of red and black clay, which turns into something that would put you in mind of an ice rink or (excuse my expression) slick as snot on a glass doorknob. We slid uncontrollably into every ditch we came near (the old song *Slip Sliding Away* came to mind more than once). Had it not been for the high lift jack that Mike insisted on carrying with us, we would probably be there until this day.

As we rounded the bend on a narrow muddy dirt path we were following through the bushes, and approached the levee lining both sides of the Sand River, I sucked in a breath and nearly gagged at the sight which lay before us. This easy moving, calm river we had crossed so many times during this three-day expedition looked like the Rio Grande having a temper tantrum—just not as deep. An unbelievable sight before our eyes! The river had swollen and the banks were slick—oh so slick! The choice we had to make seemed inescapable.

With fear and trepidation, we had to descend into the now about two-to-three-feet deep river bed, cross to the other side, and then climb the steep bank, which proved to be a grueling adventure. Mike eased the old Rover into the raging dark river water, and for a brief moment, it actually seemed we would make it. Ascending the slope that led out of the river, the old Rover started sliding back into the sullen waters. Repeatedly to no avail, he tried to get up the slippery slope. The four-wheel drive was a joke—gone, completely done for.

At the water's edge I got out of the vehicle and stood on the bank, praying for God to make a way of escape. A stunning thought wormed its way into my mind (the "what ifs"). With every failed try mingling with anticipation and perplexity, it seemed there was no way out. Funny the things that we pray about when faced with certain disaster. "Oh Lord," I whispered, "if we don't make it out of here and this is the end, please let my dad know that I want him to rejoice because I have given my life for what God has called me to do."

After countless failed attempts to crest the levee, Mike was forced to abandon our original tracks. With rising determination, he navigated the middle of the river in hopes of locating a navigable crossing, actually a way of escape in either direction.

Mikey, said, "Dad, put the car in reverse and try this slope again. Maybe the four-wheel will work in reverse."

They argued back and forth for a while about the fact that if the four-wheel were out one way, then it would be out the other. However, with no other plan to try, Mike turned it around and started up backwards. With breathless anticipation, I watched and prayed, as once again the old beast began to slide backwards down that slippery slope. My breath caught in my throat; I gasped, as Mikey placed himself in front of the vehicle, now facing the river. In one frantic moment, he heaved with all his strength against the sliding weight of metal. Prayers involuntarily exploded from my lips. I could hear my heart pounding out of my chest.

"Oh God, please help us." I was tempted to cover my eyes and not look at what could happen; but I prayed, knowing that God was our Source of divine help. "Dispatch angels to assist us. Please God, help us. Come to our rescue. Nothing is too hard for You to do."

Then as if a mighty hand came down and lifted the car, it crested the levee and made it safely to solid ground on the other side.

It took some time for my heart to stop beating like a runaway train out of control. I stood for a long moment and took in several slow deep breaths, allowing my quivering muscles to still, taking the time to thank my God, my Lord and Deliverer, for never leaving us or forsaking us. This storm did not take Him by surprise. He stores the rain, lightning, and thunder in His storehouses in heaven.

A slivered moon hung askew in the sky as we pulled out of the sand river on that adventurous night. The storm moved down the valley to weather another soul. Weary and worn, we peered at the ice chip stars that hung suspended overhead, occasionally being blocked by black clouds. It seemed as if they were at war as to which one would rule the remainder of the night. I began to let out a long-held breath, and felt that all was well with the world. However, in Africa, *every* minute can be an adventure.

As if fighting the river wasn't enough, when we rounded a hairpin bend with the thick bush closing in all around our narrow dirt path, an angrily surprised cape buffalo, unappreciative of our intrusion, charged our Rover. We narrowly escaped a collision of man versus adrenalin junkie, frightened beast. By this time, I'm not sure which was the beast: the cape buffalo, or the Rover's occupants!

Finally, as if peeping from under a black quilt, we could see the twinkle of lights announcing the presence of the Sopa Lodge looming high on the hill far in the distance. We knew that our little Hippo Camp was about a mile below those lights. Tears of joy pooled in my eyes as we gave thanks to our God for His great hand of protection and deliverance.

At about 11:00 p.m. we pulled into Hippo Camp weary, tired, and filthy dirty, not caring what creature might be creeping in our little, grass-roofed house. We were just too tired to give it any thought—after I checked the place out with a flashlight.

Prayers flowed freely concerning the lost people of Loita over the course of the next few days. God is not willing that *any* should perish, but that *all* would come to repentance. If God is not willing, then neither am I. One day kingdom critical mass will be achieved, and then Jesus will come to take His bride to live with Him for eternity. Just maybe one more salvation in the Loita Hills would produce critical mass for the Lord's return—*until the whole world knows*. The call deep within my heart is to reach each and every person with the good news that Jesus saves. There was much ministry to complete before we could take a break and fly to the United States.

As the days passed, and the ground dried up while traveling to others villages to minister, we

crossed the same place where we had been stranded. The riverbed was powder-puff dry. As we gawked at the place where earlier we had fought for our very lives, we had to give thanks to our Heavenly Father. We were acutely aware of His divine protection, for there were impassably huge boulders, three and four-feet in diameter that filled the riverbed where Mike had driven back and forth trying to find a way of escape. There was no way he could have crossed them in the natural realm. We knew God had supernaturally intervened and delivered us once again. It was great to see with our own eyes just what God had done for us.

The time had now come for us to return to the States for a short period of time, with the hopes of completing necessary preparations that would assist us in the ministry of preaching the gospel to the Maasai of Loita Hills. We set to work on booking tents and cooks, and mapping better routes for travel.

Mike and I had given up trying to pastor and do missions at the same time; however, as preachers, if we don't preach, then we don't eat. We had revivals scheduled in the States, and Mike felt he could not cancel these services as we desperately needed the funds to support the ministry of soul winning.

We agreed that Mikey, our son, and I would return to Loita with tents and set up a camp in this unreached area. The only way to allow extended time for ministry in such a remote area would be old-fashioned camping.

Mike made the decision to remain in the States to preach revivals and raise the necessary funds to support this outreach.

Mikey and I boarded the big bird that would carry us back to the Dark Continent once again—as ready as we would ever be to head out into the unknown for the gospel's sake.

Nearly three months had passed since we had first heard of the need in Loita, and we had made a commitment to the people to bring the gospel. Visions given to us supernaturally were now taking shape and coming to life. Mikey and I hired tents and a cook from a company called *Across Africa Safaris* (supposedly a reputable outfit but as today's youth say, "NOT!") We had mapped a better route to get into the Loitas, and hired a second vehicle and driver. There were several brave souls from America with us who had hearts like ours to reach the unreached—whatever the cost. Among this band of soldiers were Pastor Louis and Jane Sullivan, Cheryl Wood, and Judy Myrick.

Across Africa Safaris said the tents they had packed for us were two-man tents and cost only $28.00 a night per person. It sounded great, but as with most things in Africa, it was not what they had claimed it to be. But we did not find that out until we were setting up camp in Loita after dark— too far to turn back and demand a refund. We could do nothing about their lie.

With all the treacherous paths behind us, the dream of bringing the gospel to Loita was now becoming a reality. Our bodies were longing to stop bouncing and get horizontal. We ached to crawl into our blankets for a good night's sleep, but this would not be the case. There were more challenging adventures on the horizon.

Mikey and I gaped in horror as our eyes scrutinized the grounds covered with thigh-high grass. We had been told this was a great campsite. My personal thoughts spun a *"could be"* tale of horror. "Oh, dear God!" Goose bumps crawled up and down my neck and spine.

For the next few suspended minutes, unspoken words reverberated between Mikey and me, sending the same message of concern. Each of us thoroughly understood the other's silent warnings. In unison we said, "This is not a good idea," which translated meant, *"No way are we going to set up tents in this three-foot-high grass."* We would be fair game for leopards, lions, snakes, and only God knows what else.

No, we would find another location more suitable with shorter grass, which helped a little with security. We needed to be able to see what was out and about. We needed a location to camp, one where the peace of God would let us know we had selected rightly; not one where certain danger lurked in the grass. Thoughts whirled as we kept driving around the area, carefully screening the surrounding shadows, until about a mile away we found a place where the grass was much shorter, making us feel considerably better. Having never been in this remote bush area before, we felt the first order of business was to start a fire to light up the place and lend some protection against whatever the local wild life there may be.

A long night doesn't even begin to describe what we were about to experience. As we warmed ourselves by the fire, we pushed down unnerving feelings of the *"what ifs."* The memories of the craziness of trusting only our guides while driving on no roads seemed to dwindle away. A backdrop of a gorgeous African sky and the fire's flames chased away weariness as it flickered across the tired, dirty little faces at our camp. The fire warmed our chilled bodies. I was so tired I hardly remember eating the plate of spaghetti our cook had prepared. Huddled as closely to the fire as we dare, we ate from plates placed on our laps. We could hear hyenas and many other unidentifiable animal sounds, but soon we would become experts on all the strange night noises. The fire was warming and comforting. Had we not been so tired, I don't think any of us would have left the soothing protection of the fire that first night. However, all these warm cuddly feelings would soon take flight like a bird destined to reach the south before winter.

We were all experiencing jet lag, which made us dizzy-headed, so very tired, and a little addled. Actually, jet lag is like half the body is in one place, but finds the other half in another.

When the guys we had hired to bring the tents and set them up began staking them into the ground, I glanced over my shoulder at the commotion and instantly knew we had been scammed. The tents may have been as tall as my shoulder. When lying, my head touched one end and my feet pushed on the zipper at the other end—if left unzipped, my feet would protruded into the great outdoors. Now that's some real protection! You can only imagine the mental images in my mind as I thought of doing so. "*Oh Lord, help us all to live through this experience.*" Mikey and I argued with the men that these surely were not the tents we had booked, but arguing was a waste of time. No turning back now. For the morale of the team, we kept a strong front as if all was just as planned. If we exhibited fear or unpleasantness, it would grow like a grass fire across the plains fueled by hot winds in dry season.

We eventually left the comforts of the warm fire, and stooped down to enter the Boy Scout type tents we would call home for the next two weeks. I surrendered my suitcase to live under a nearby tree since both of us could not get into this tent at the same time. I couldn't even sit up straight to put my clothes on. Have you ever seen the commercial of a woman lying on her bed trying to wiggle into tight jeans? Of course, I wore skirts so as not to offend the natives, but dressing while lying wiggling on the ground made for lots of laughs. I learned a long time ago it's better to laugh at yourself rather than to cry. We constantly reminded ourselves why we had made this wild journey. Isn't one soul worth all the effort? *Until The Whole World Knows!*

Night took its chilling grip when we moved away from the fire to our disgustingly minuscule, expensive tents, and we became increasing more frigid as the night progressed. My own chattering teeth woke me in the middle of the bone-chilling night. I slept fitfully while dreaming of wild drives under eerie darkness, and potholes deeper than our vehicle. In desperation for warm cover, I took everything handy—boots, makeup bag, etc.—and laid them across my body. We were freezing cold. We had no cots, floor mats, blankets, or even a coat. Why would we need heavy blankets? This is Africa; it is supposed to be hot. Boy, was I wrong! In my effort to pack lightly, I had packed a lap throw, much like the airlines give out in economy seating on an international flight.

We knew space would be extremely limited, so we had all brought small duffle bags for our luggage. I was at least blessed to have luggage; Mikey had none. I simply did not realize that at over 7,000 feet above sea level during the month of July, Kenya's coldest month, it can get so cold that your teeth could chatter as mine did. The old saying really is true, "There is no teacher like experience."

Early the next morning, while sitting around the fire eating from the plates held in our laps, and trying to thaw out from the bitter night's cold, we talked about ways to be warmer during the night since we had limited covers. Someone suggested that if we had plastic tablecloths, it would help retain our body heat. Bingo! I had brought a twin plastic mattress cover just in case I had to stay in a bug-infested bed. I have had too many experiences with that sort of thing to ever leave home without one. It's part of my luggage, like a toothbrush or hairbrush.

Once when preaching in Turkana country, we stayed in the only place available. It was terribly infested with bats, rats, roaches, huge monstrous flying grasshoppers of Biblical proportion, with large bugs in the bed mattress made of straw. I emptied a giant can of bug spray, and still it was alive. Crawling insects laid within the folds that made up the mattress. One tends to remember these incidents. From that time to this, the mattress cover is a part of my packing list. Mikey found a Maasai market and bought all the blankets they had available, but there weren't enough to go around. It didn't worry me because I had a new plan. That night I wrapped myself in my little lap throw and scooted down into my plastic bed liner, and much to my pleasant surprise, it held my body heat. There were no more nights of waking up to my teeth chattering.

The first night was pretty miserable and dangerous on so many levels. When I woke with my teeth chattering, I needed to go to the bathroom. I unzipped my tent and whispered, "Cheryl." Cheryl Wood is a dear friend from South Louisiana where we had pastored for ten years.

I heard her from inside her tent say, "Yeah."

I said, "I have to answer nature's call."

I didn't even have to ask her to accompany me; she just replied, "I'm coming."

We quietly slipped out of our tents into the cold black night. I looked toward the fire where our only night guard curled in a deep sleep near the warm flickering glow. In my inexperience, I was excited that he was asleep so I wouldn't have to go so far from camp to relieve myself. I had planned to walk a couple of hundred yards away where we had a makeshift toilet—nothing more than a hole in the ground—but when I stepped out into the night, I felt eyes watching my every move, and my feelings were later justified. That little catching of my breath in anticipation of lurking danger nibbled away at my comfort zone. A voice inside of my head very strongly encouraged me to refrain from stepping out into the shadows.

Cheryl stood guard while I answered nature's call. We managed to slip back into our tents without awaking anyone else, including the sleeping Maasai night guard, until we zipped the tents closed. Moses Ole Sayo, our dear Maasai friend, awoke and stepped out into the sullen night to wake the slumbering guard. He immediately became aware of the sinister presence of a large leopard within our modest camp.

The leopard (*chui*—its Swahili name) is one of the most elusive, powerful, clever, and dangerous animals in the world today. A large *chui* is anything over 115 pounds and six and one-half feet in length. This one was huge—the size of a lioness. I've never seen a larger leopard anywhere. It is a proven fact that a leopard is capable of killing prey more than three times its size. He will carry it a long distance, then drag it into a tree for safekeeping from other predators or scavengers. Leopards are not afraid of man as some would have you to believe. They are known to enjoy the delightful taste of humans. Known as casual killers, they are cunningly fast and bold.

The Maasai will tell you that leopards eat people as part of their normal diet. Man is just another item on their food chain. Without moving a steely muscle, a hungry leopard will lay waiting for hours, calculating an attack of death, which is as fast as a streak of lightning. I have heard it said, "They are a perfect killing machine." Leopards are incredibly strong and move with blinding speed; shy and nocturnal, but unafraid of men. Leopards live near the villages of men, killing anything that they jolly well want to—cows, sheep, and children. Camouflaged with their blending beautiful slick coats, they are hard-core killers. It takes just one mistake, one night alone, one moment within the reach of the leopard's paw, and God, and God alone to save you from certain death. I do live on the premise, however, "Until God is finished with you, you are immortal," quoted to me by my son, Mikey, when he faced terminal cancer.

The hand of the Lord protected us when we slipped out of our tent to answer nature's call.

Later during that night of increasing trepidation, I awoke to the most horrible, obnoxious stench wafting into my tent. It smelled like dead rotting flesh. It was so insulting to my nostrils that I sat up, my head touching the top of the tent. When I looked toward the fire that Sayo had made and which later the night guard built larger, I saw a hyena silhouetted larger than normal, rubbing its nasty, odor-filled fur against my tent.

One night at another ministry camp a hyena stood under the pressure lamp and cried out its eerie wailing sound. They are supposed to run from light or fire, but some hyenas didn't get that memo! Contrary to the belief that they are scavengers, the hyena kills over eighty percent of its food. Just two nights before, hyenas killed 87 goats and sheep and scattered 150 others where we were camping. Before too many days, I would come to recognize all the savage sounds of this nasty smelling beast. I have learned to listen to them every night and let them lull me to sleep with their creepy savage songs that have come to represent the death and life of the bushland to me.

Needless to say, I didn't sleep anymore that night. Since that time we have more than one night guard and more than one fire for protection. I feel for sure that God had assigned many warrior angels to protect us from dangers that only eternity will reveal. I can hardly wait to hear, as Paul Harvey was famous for saying, "The rest of the story."

On Monday evening at about 10:00 p.m.—pitch dark on the equator—nature called Mikey. In these moments, one often hopes the sensation goes away so the sweet embrace of sleep will return; this was not the case. We laughingly commented that Mikey wore his tent—because the tents were so small. Rather than crawl inside and wiggle out, Mikey slipped his on and off. He stood, removed his tent, and stretched in the brisk night air.

When working among the Maasai, it is good practice to look the part, complete with shuka, sword, and sheath. Mikey often tried to make the Maasai shuka—a wool blanket the Maasai wear over their shoulder which they use for everything from cover to clothing—work for him. But I have never seen a Maasai who looked like Mikey because of his skin color and shape. Mikey was by far the largest guy on the team; no one's clothes even came close to fitting his thunder thighs. Since our luggage had as yet to arrive after a couple of days, he finally tied a red and blue-checkered shuka around his waist and wore it as a skirt, appearing much like a Samoan lost in the bush. However, Mikey had become inseparable from his blade when in the bush country due to several experiences, and tonight was no exception.

Whenever one is in a place as dangerous as this, the body's senses go into overdrive. Hearing, smell, and sight run on high alert to assist in the preservation of one's life. Peering into the darkness, Mikey could make out the silhouette of the tree line that marked the beginning of the dense forest near our camp. "It's good enough for the animals, so it is for me, too," he mumbled under his breath.

About this time, another guy on the team rose up from the mouth of his tent and stretched. Nature was evidently busy about her calls this evening. Mikey whispered over to him, "You okay?" He said he was and started heading towards the established latrine for the camp. Mikey walked over to meet him, diverting his path from the dense wood.

Meeting up on the path to the latrine, Mikey and his buddy began to talk about the joys of sleeping in these *wonderful* conditions when silence struck them . . . something was out there! Their senses, honed to a razor's edge, had caught a faint disturbance. The one who didn't wish to be discovered made his move. Turning their lights in perfect unison as if alarms had gone off that danger was at hand, the beams fell into the eyes of a spotted bullet of fur and teeth, exploding from the forest where Mikey was originally headed. *"Chui!"* The leopard streaked in a blur totally invested in killing the two servants of Jesus caught outside the safety of the campfire's glow.

With the fluid motion of a trained warrior, Mikey pulled his Maasai sword free of its covering, borne out by the adrenalin gushing forth to give the body a chance to live. Rick, who had had more than a little trouble working the leather sheath off his blade earlier, had no trouble wrestling it free in this moment. Bracing for the battle that would end in life or death, and absolutely no less, Mikey uttered under his breath, "This is going to hurt."

The leopard closed the distance impossibly fast, with the desperate need to fill its belly with human flesh. At the last moment, when the beast would trade the ground for air and leap upon his victims, a desperate prayer escaped my son's lips. Prayers in a moment such as this often lack the sophistication of one that is prepared. No time to add *"Our Father"* and *"Beseech You, O Holy One"*; no *"Thees"* and *"Thines."* Just desperate words born out of sheer terror, "Jesus, help us!"

As if time itself was submitting to the arrival of its Maker, everything slowed down. Mikey watched the claws digging in to surge forward. The blur of the beast had gone into full detail, with each hair's outline contrasting against the other. The body seemed to want to record in perfect detail every moment for the retelling of its final breath.

It was at this point that something out of the ordinary realm happened in the form of *a dog*. A dog, man's best friend and humble companion, appeared out of the night, hurling itself at the great cat. The leopard was caught unaware. This should not happen; a leopard's greatest tool is his stealth. To be spotted is to lose, and he knows it. Yet, here the beast was met with surprise. The dog barked and growled and lunged and bit the air as one fighting for the well-being of his oldest friend. Shock and automatic response caused the leopard to abandon his human prey and make flight away from this audacious canine.

Mikey stood motionless in awe of how the moment had changed. Looking at the place where there was certain death one hurried breath before, there now stood the dog. Mikey was unsure if his situation had improved. After all, a forty-pound *"bow wow"* had just frightened away two-hundred pounds of hungry *"meow, meow!"* That was one bad dog! The little dog stared out into the night where the leopard had run bristling.

"He looked over at us, then back after the leopard, whereupon he simply disappeared. He didn't slip off into the night, nor did our light just not illuminate his path. One moment he was in our light's beam, and the next he was gone." Mikey recounted to me the story with a smile on his face, saying, "At that point I didn't need to go to the restroom anymore; however, I did need to change my pants."

The next morning Mikey took some of the Maasai over to the place of the attack. These men live by knowing the land and being able to read its signs. They found the leopard's hiding place where it had watched the camp for several days. They found where it had rushed out to take my son as prey. They found where it turned from its assault and ran away. However, what could not be found nor explained in mortal terms was where the dog had come from. It was as if he was never there. Mikey laughed and noted that this was proof that dogs do go to heaven. It was obvious an angel had come; the Saviour had heard my son's desperate prayer. We could not know that our fortune would lead to a revival of Biblical proportions in the Loita Hills.

We had made it through five days without our luggage, but the time came for us to try to retrieve it. Before we had ventured away from Jomo Kenyatta Airport in Nairobi, we had arranged for the luggage to be flown to the nearest airstrip at Keekorok Lodge in the Maasai Mara Game Reserve the next day. If you believe that our bags would arrive the next day, then I have ocean front property in Arizona to sell you. It is not uncommon to lose your luggage forever when its destination is Kenya.

On one occasion, I asked the airlines to book me on the route that my luggage—a three-foot carved teakwood giraffe packed in a box—had taken. It had gone to Paris, England, and Germany before arriving in the USA. My giraffe had the more interesting flight schedule! Now we were once again in one country, and our luggage was in a mystery location. We had given the airlines a week to locate the errant bags.

Before dawn, the morning after Mikey's dreadful encounter with the leopard, we began the challenging journey over the mountains to Keekorok. We dreaded the trip, but felt we had no other choice, praying and trusting that miraculously somehow our bags had been safely delivered to Keekorok's dirt airstrip, which was about six hours one way over a bad dirt path. We were leaving behind a leopard, which with no doubt was watching our every move.

After the leopard's failed attempt on our team, he retreated from our camp. Under the covering of the dark night, this overgrown spotted streak of death, moving like lightning whipping across the sky, continued his quest for food. With his keen night vision, he spotted three Maasai men keeping a vigil over their sheep. The men were completely unaware of approaching death. Leopards are very patient hunters, often waiting for hours, motionless on their haunches, ready to take purpose and launch an attack.

Dawn was slowly bleeding over the skies when the waiting, calculating leopard made his move against the herd. You may think that leopards are not a serious matter to contend with; however, some leopards have earned man-eating status, recording as many as 400 victims for one leopard. This *chui* must have desired to add notches in his belt to seek out the well-guarded animals. He launched his killing massacre on the herd, and found himself pursued by the angry, fearless shepherds.

Maasai will lay down their lives to protect their livestock. From childhood, they're taught bravery and the arts of protecting their families and animals from predators.

The *chui* attacked all three men at once, wounding all of them. Since a leopard wraps his arms around a body and guts it with his claws, his teeth and talons buried into one man's head. All three men were fighting with this one determined leopard. He buried his teeth deep into their flesh. He made his mistake when deciding to finish one man off before proceeding to dispatch the others.

Maasai are brave fighters and will not back down or run from such a fight. While the leopard held his chosen victim in a death grip with his teeth, his talons clawing at his head and other extremities, one of the other Maasai managed to decapitate the leopard with his sword. The Maasai men had to cut out the leopard's teeth one at a time to free its helpless victim—their friend. His arm had a gaping hole that an orange could easily pass through. His head, forearms, and legs had huge bite and claw marks. However, this killer would kill no more. He had picked the wrong menu for breakfast.

All three Maasai were injured, but one was critical. When we left to pick up luggage, several team members remained at the camp. When the wounded were brought to their attention, they did all that they could do to help.

A retired anesthesiologist on our team, well versed in emergency care, was able to do some makeshift patch-up work. The danger now was blood poisoning from the leopard's teeth and claws. Raw meat is their steady diet, making the teeth and claws lethal weapons of sepsis. After doing all that they could to clean the wounds, our team decided to make a bed for the man in the back of the old green truck, and take him to a rural medical station rumored to be in the area. When they arrived, there was nothing with which to treat the man. They gave the acting nurse—who was probably not a nurse at all—money and said, "We cannot take this man any further; however, we are leaving you with the money to get this man to a clinic that can treat his wounds."

After arrangements were made, the team headed back for camp. The injured man was left in the hands of a nurse out in the middle of nowhere. Little did we know that this act of kindness would open the door to present the gospel of Jesus Christ. He does work in mysterious ways, His wonders to perform.

Hot and dusty, we arrived at Keekorok in the early afternoon and were sorely disappointed. No luggage awaited us.

We headed back to Loita by way of Siana Springs tented camp a few miles outside of the reserve, which also had a dirt airstrip. We thought that, by some far out chance, the airlines might have dropped the luggage at the Siana Springs. I shared a soda and visited with the manager—an old friend of mine—for a while, and he assured me that no one had delivered luggage to him. We were about to leave when he said, "Marigold, come with me and let's go check the air strip. Maybe someone dropped the luggage without notifying me. There was a plane that landed earlier today." I jumped into his large open land cruiser—designed for better game viewing—and we took off on the dirt path, leaving what looked like a dust storm in our wake, as we headed for the airstrip.

When we rounded the curve approaching the airstrip, I caught a glimpse of a stack of luggage neatly sitting in the middle of the dirt runway, undisturbed by the many animals around it or the Maasai who had to walk by it. There it was, just waiting for its owners to come and claim it. Praise the Lord for His many blessings! Had we come a day earlier, we would have missed it, or had we come a day later, it could have been stolen or damaged by the wild animals. God is so good!

We thankfully collected the luggage and started the long dusty, hard journey back to our little camp nestled in the Loita Hills. It was well after dark when we finally rolled to a stop at the tents.

The talk around the fire that night was non-stop excitement as we were informed about the leopard attack on the Maasai, and we told what a miracle it was that we actually found our luggage without cell phones to track it down. It gave me pause to realize just what danger we were in with the large *chui* stalking.

As the sun began its silent ascent across the horizon the following morning, two Maasai Morani runners (warriors) entered our camp and invited us to come to the celebration of a newly appointed chief. We were so excited to be a part of such a memorable event. Before 8:00 a.m., we slowly drove to the village as instructed. Some of the Morani came up to the car, looking curiously at themselves in the side mirrors. It was fascinating to witness their marveling at their images in the mirror, as if they had never before seen anything like a mirror or their reflections.

The Maasai were so wild and their countenances revealed unequivocally *that they were not saved and knew nothing of Jesus*. The first thought that came to my mind was, *"Do I dare open this door and get out of the safety of this car?"* They all seemed so intimidating, but weren't *they* the reason we came? *They* were why we stayed in dinky little tents in the middle of the wild African bush. No one ever said it would be easy.

I was quite taken by their body paintings, braided long red clay-dyed hair, short cloths around the midriff that make miniskirts look long, and dangling earlobes. Their bodies were painted from the bottom of the feet to the top of their heads. When we arrived, they were painting one another and grooming each other's hair. I'm quite sure as they beheld the likes of us they were just as entertained. With great trepidation, I eased the door open and stepped out onto their turf, fully aware that we were intruders into their celebration.

There were hundreds of men sitting on the slight slope with red paint on their faces, arms, and legs as previously described. Their pierced earlobes had been stretched large enough one could pass a good-sized orange through. Some of the men even had large pieces of wood in their ears, stretching them out even longer. Some wore rings in those ears and beads around their necks, legs—just below the knee—and arms—just above the elbow. They had what looked like cigar burns running down their arms. A few women were there only to serve the men. It was a man's day; of this you can be sure. We awkwardly stood around watching all the commotion.

The newly appointed chief made his way over to me and said, "Now you do what you have come here to do." So we set up our little PA system and began to sing, testify, and preach. He allowed us about 30 to 40 minutes, then said; "Now it is our turn."

They danced and spit milk on the ground, which I later learned was their traditional way to give drink to their dead loved ones. They chanted, jumped, and told stories in Maasai songs. After some time the young chief returned to me and said, "Now it is your turn."

Once again, we sang, preached, and encouraged them to accept this message of Jesus, the Son of the Living God. Our day went this way from 8:00 am to 6:00 p.m.—back and forth; back and forth.

At the end of the day he said to the more than 400 elders, "These people are from Engai (God). They saved the life of my father-in-law yesterday who was nearly killed by a leopard; and we will hear what they have come to say. They are good people."

This was the first time we had heard about the leopard attack playing a part in our invitation to the inauguration of the new chief. We knew in our hearts that God had orchestrated the entire saga.

Once again we gave a message of Jesus' saving love. The chief gave us a goat in appreciation for saving his father-in-law's life. He said to me, "I give you land; please build your *boma* here on this land." A *boma* is a house made of mud and sticks lined with cow dung.

I said, "Chief, I can't build a *boma*, but I can build a church here."

He said, "What is a church?"

I was stunned: perhaps I should not have been, but I was. I proceeded to explain to the chief that a church was a place for them to come together and learn more about God and His Son who died for our transgressions.

He replied, "Then we will build a church." For obvious reasons, we named it "Big Cat Assembly of God!"

By the end of the week, over 800 Maasai, mostly men, and a few women had accepted Jesus as Lord of their lives, and eighteen had been filled with the Holy Spirit. There was no question that God had ordained this ministry time.

One evening, a *libones*—a witch doctor's son—came to our camp seeking help from evil spirits. We noticed the enormous amount of witchcraft paraphernalia called juju around his neck. We explained the way of salvation, and suggested that he throw his juju in the fire. He sat there like a zombie, not closing his eyes, not praying with us at all. I decided to walk away and worship the Lord. I felt a spirit of praise come upon me.

I thanked God for the beautiful starlit night, and knew how David must have felt when he no doubt lay on his back and worshiped the God of the heavens and marveled at His handiwork. Soon I was praying in the Spirit. I could feel God so near. The night guard walked up beside me. I was vaguely aware of his presence. I felt led of God to break my rule regarding touching men, and laid my hands on his shoulder and prayed for him to come to know the saving knowledge of Jesus. He fell on his face in the cold dirt and began to worship. He lay prostrate on the ground before the Lord of the heavens and earth, and began to speak in a heavenly language as the Spirit of God moved upon him.

I marveled at how wonderfully awesome this beautiful sight was. Then I was strangely drawn back to the fire where, at first, I did not see our visitor who had come for help. But then I saw him. He had removed his juju and thrown it into the fire, and he, too, was lying prostrate—face down—in the dirt by the fire praising God for opening his eyes to the understanding of who Jesus is. It was a glorious evening of praising God under the stars.

Many would say the dangers and inconveniences outweighed any good that would come from that trip; but I say that would be a completely wrong-headed notion. If it were easy, everyone would do it. It isn't easy, but it is wonderfully rewarding.

The church, *Big Cat Assembly of God,* is doing extremely well. The night guard is now a preacher of the Word and more than half of our Loita Hills pastors were once *libones*—witch doctors. There are now nearly 100 Kenya Assemblies of God— KAG —Churches in Loita. Literally thousands of Loita Maasai are born again, Spirit-filled believers. Praise God!

One year after our initial ministry in Loita Hills, we returned for more ministry time. A man walked up to me and asked, "Do you remember me?" I struggled pulling up his face in my memory bank.

Realizing my dilemma, he said, "I was the man who crawled up to hear you tell us about God having a Son. I had been crippled for years from Brucellosis. That day I believed and ask Jesus to be Lord of my life. You prayed for me to be helped, as well; then you drove away. What you did not know was when you drove away I got up and walked away. God not only forgave my transgressions. He healed my body that very day when you prayed for me. I have been watching and waiting for you to return so that I could tell you my good news."

We were within the leopard's reach, but once again, God came to our rescue. Romans chapter eight tells us that He has reserved the right to take the schemes of hell and turn them into part of the blueprint of the glorious dominion of the kingdom of God.

5
DARE TO HOPE

Mikey's Story

5

DARE TO HOPE

Mikey's Story

"**A**re you threatening me with *heaven*? Heaven is no threat to me," said Mikey, our son, bravely to his doctor.

The doctor replied, "I may have a twenty-percent chance of saving your life if you will let me treat you. Otherwise, you won't live."

"I want a miracle from God," Mikey said.

"That's a rare thing," the doctor responded.

"Well, I'll believe God for that rare miracle then," stated Mikey.

"I'll have the port for chemo taken out," the doctor announced.

"Thanks," Mikey said.

With an expression of defeat, the doctor sadly walked out of Mikey's room. I'm sure he felt that he was Mikey's only hope.

Once the doctor left, the attending nurse turned and said to Mikey, "Can I hug you?" Before he could respond, she held him in a bear hug with tears flowing freely down her face as she cried.

When they had all vacated the room, Mikey turned to me. "I guess that was foolish for me to refuse more chemo, wasn't it, Mom?"

I had kept silent during the whole ordeal. Standing in the corner of the hospital room, I had tried to remain invisible, which is a miracle in itself for me or any other mother when her son faces certain death.

I slipped over to Mikey's side and said, "No, son. This morning in prayer, the Lord spoke to me that you would be breathing and living by faith."

I consider myself blessed to have a family that is very close and who genuinely love each other. My beautiful daughter Melissa, seven years older than her brother, Mikey, is always looking out for him, like big sisters do.

One day she said, "Mom, you need to check out a lump on Mikey's neck."

I said, "Thanks, I'll do that," and that day I made a point of finding him to see this lump about which both Melissa and his wife, Shereen, had spoken. Much to my chagrin, they were right. A large lump, not in a gland, was clearly apparent in Mikey's neck region.

"Son," I said, "You *must* have this checked." He argued that he didn't have a doctor.

I said, "If you love me, you will find one and check this out. I'm not happy about the appearance of this lump."

I guess he still loves his mom, because he searched for a doctor with whom he wouldn't have to wait for an appointment. He found a new physician just starting her practice with no patient list. Since Mikey was one of her first patients, she wanted to be very thorough.

After examining him, she said, "I'd like to take an x-ray to rule out pneumonia." Mikey said that was no problem. Like a kid, he sat on the end of the exam table playing with a sectional larynx display as he waited for the x-ray results.

The doctor walked into his room with tears visibly pooled in her eyes. She sat down in front of him. Looking deep into his face scarred from burns he had suffered years before, she gazed into his deep blue eyes as if asking the question, *Can you handle what I need to say to you?* She took a long breath and carefully chose her words. "You look like you've been through a lot in your life, so maybe you can handle what I have to tell you."

Mikey sat swinging his feet trying to anticipate what in the world this lady was trying to say to him. Holding up the film, she continued, "See this x-ray? This is where we should be able to see your heart . . . and here your lungs and over here, your organs. But as you can see, we can see nothing but this mass."

"Hum, okay," Mikey said a bit awkwardly.

As tears rolled down her cheeks, she said, "I've never had to tell anyone this before. You are dying, and it may only be two weeks."

Mikey sat on the bed bewildered, stunned. He was unsure of what to say to this physician who was obviously distraught, and uncertain of appropriate words.

He simply said, "Okay."

Thoughts flooded Mikey's mind. *"What should he do next?"* Looking at the doctor who was still standing there, every bit as awkward as he was, Mikey asked if he could take the x-ray with him. The doctor agreed.

While putting on his shirt in preparation to leave, Mikey wondered how to tell Shereen, his beautiful wife of only two months, that she was going to be a widow.

With the x-ray under his arm, Mikey headed out of the office, and wandered his way to his car. Much like a man having had one too many, he had difficulty working the key into the door of the vehicle. All at once, a resolve entered into his heart. Taking his phone from his pocket, he dialed the familiar number of my cell phone. Mikey said to himself in a morbid humor, "This is Mom's fault anyway, since she made me go to the doctor." Turning out of the parking lot, Mikey headed into one more journey of uncertainty that could cost him his life.

That afternoon we met—Mikey with his x-ray in tow. He held it up to the sun so we could clearly see the results and said, "Well, Mom, if this is true, I am a dead man."

His chest organs were completely blocked out by a huge white mass. I could not see his heart or lungs. A thought crashed in my head like a tree downed in a storm. *"Was it even possible that this could be a true reading?"* However, at that moment, I could not allow myself to even entertain the thought.

I waved my hand in dismissal and said, "This must be a fluke, or the machine is malfunctioning, or some other strange phenomenon, or something like that. It can't be a true x-ray. I've never seen anything like this." Grasping to understand, I continued, "I know, the devil put his ugly hand in front of the x-ray, making this look like a mass in order to scare all of us."

Later that day we went into Ryan's Restaurant, refusing to believe this crazy report. However, my heart ached for my son, and I could not help but ponder what challenges the future would hold for all of us.

I wasted no time calling Mike, my husband, who was preaching a revival in Virginia. He immediately started fasting. For the next eight days, he prayed and fasted, believing God for a miracle. On the eighth day, he began to pray in a language that he had never prayed in before, and felt he was in deep intercession for Mikey's life.

At this stage in the game, I was in complete denial—rejecting the sick feeling which was squeezing my stomach like a vise grip. I tried to fully believe it was a broken machine that had regurgitated this demonic lie. I said to myself, "*It was an x-ray that was all snow white. It simply could not be for real. Yes, the machine had to be broken. No other explanation would do. Why would the doctor give him such a worthless x-ray?*"

The more I reflected on this x-ray from hell, the more I convinced myself that it was somehow flawed with no possible validity. Yet, what was this shiver crawling up and down my spine? Why was I tossing and turning in a fitful sleep, sometimes sitting straight up as if I'd heard a loud clatter?

The doctor that had seen Mikey sent him to an ear, nose, and throat specialist. Upon arrival, they informed Mikey and Shereen they had overbooked their schedule and simply could not see him for two weeks.

Mikey said, "No problem," and started toward the door. He was adamant that he didn't want to be doing this stuff anyway.

However, his new bride, Shereen, heard the exchange and whispered under her breath, "This is a problem."

As Mikey headed away, he heard a commotion and turned to see what was happening. Shereen slapped both hands loudly on the counter, leaned into the nurse's face, she said with all the passion of someone in love and scared to death, "We don't have that kind of time!" The veins in

Shereen's face were clearly visible and her intensity unquestionable. The nurse slid her chair backward against the wall. *(I love Shereen like a daughter, but that day, I loved her for being a Florence Nightingale, an Esther, a heroine on Mikey's behalf.)*

Shereen explained the size of the mass in his chest, and within a few minutes, she had them convinced to see him immediately. There's nothing quite as persuasive as a new wife who is facing the realization that her husband could actually be dying! Within thirty minutes, he was with the doctor; and the next morning, he was in the hospital for a biopsy of one tumor in his neck area.

As they rolled him into surgery from his hospital room, he was sitting up cross-legged on his gurney. He refused to be put to sleep because it would require an endotracheal intubation. You see, during his recovery from severe burns as a child, he wore a trachea for seven years. He was adamant about not ever wearing one again.

En route to the operating room, he had the gurney driver stop so that he could pray with another patient—a man going in for knee replacement surgery. *(That's Mikey, always thinking of others!)*

Arriving in the prepared surgical room alert and awake due to receiving no anesthesia, Mikey had two requests. He asked the surgeon to allow him to pray for him before they began the procedure, and he requested praise music to be played in the operating room during surgery. The kind surgeon obliged him these requests. Mikey was fully awake for the procedures.

Adam, our son-in-law, was interning at medical school and was therefore allowed to shadow Mikey's surgery. When the surgeon tried to remove the tumor in Mikey's neck, he found tentacles attached to the tumor running to other areas; so, they had to just cut it off. If you know anything about the nature of cancer, then you know that this is a terrible thing to do.

We anxiously awaited the results. As soon as the procedure was complete, the doctor said Mikey needed immediate radiation therapy. Mexican food seemed to be calling his name, so before we all rushed over for radiation, the whole family decided to drown our disappointments and anxiety in bowls of quesadilla dip, salsa, and enchiladas. We finished our Mexican extravaganza which none of us tasted; no one wanted to mention the *elephant in the room*, in hopes this was all just a bad dream.

I gasped when Mikey walked out of the radiation room with red x's on his chest, his body marked for treatment. At the realization of the magnitude of his condition, all color drained from my face. It was as if I had been hit in the face with a sledgehammer. His entire chest and neck was marked up with lines and x's.

When the doctor explained the results of his findings, the words sucked the very breath from my body. It was as if I was hearing, but not hearing. I wanted to put my hands over my ears and say, *"Stop this! I don't want to hear you. You are wrong! Don't say another word!"* However, the unwelcome verdict continued to spill over my soul like rancid water from a contaminated spring. Couldn't he see that he was giving us a death sentence for Mikey?

I had the cancer, not my child. It was one thing for *me*, but it was absolutely unacceptable for my baby. If someone needed to have this deadly condition, let it be me, not my son. *"Be strong, Marigold,"* I told myself. *"Mikey needs you to be courageous, fearless."*

As the reports kept coming, I silently prayed, *"Oh, God, help me. I am not fearless or strong without You. God, this is my son, my baby! Help me to not pass out. Help my legs to hold me up as I listen to these dreaded words."*

The doctor explained that the cancerous tumor in our son's chest was already twenty-one inches long, fifteen inches wide, five and one-half inches thick, and was growing one-half inch per day. He also had multiple golf-ball-size tumors throughout his body, all malignant. Medically, it was a hopeless situation. Of course, to confirm this report, they needed to take one of the tumors for full testing. They chose the one in his neck.

They administered CT, PET, and bone scans. After the terrible results, they hospitalized Mikey, not expecting him to live.

I stormed into my house and fell, as one assassinated, onto my knees in my living room where I love to pray. I made my square leather hassock an altar, desperate to hear from God. My chest exploded within me. My mind reeled like a drunk on a Saturday night binge. The intense desperation within my spirit was simply indescribable! I felt for sure I would implode from within. The sick feeling in the pit of my stomach churned sour liquid, and feelings of heart failure only intensified. My knuckles and joints ached as if I had a high fever. Disaster and sorrow wrapped my breathless soul in their ugly dark talons. I knew that without a word from God, I would simply collapse from the weight of the emotional suffering.

I can remember thinking, "If I could just touch God! If only I could only know His heart and plan in this crisis! I must press through and touch the hem of His garment like the lady with the issue of blood. I simply must hear from God!"

"God, You spared this boy at eight years of age from a tragic severe burn. He died five times, and You brought him back. For what? Are You going to take him now in the prime of his life, after he has taken a wife? He's in the beginning of his ministry, and he loves You. He is a good son. He's Your follower. I don't understand. Please, Lord, speak to me. Help me to understand this! Please, God! I can't deal with this on my own. Speak to me, Lord. Speak to me!"

I cried out in wrenching anguish that only those who have walked with a precious loved one into the valley of the shadow of death can relate. I cried from deeper depths than I knew existed. A well of pure sorrow swelled up and out, exploding like lava from a volcano. Fighting to put my thoughts into prayers, I continued to call out to the only One with the power to help; the One who holds life and death in the palm of His mighty hand.

"Lord, we are on speaking terms. Let me know something, anything, whatever it is. Just let me hear from You, oh, Jesus, please!"

With these pleading words still on my lips, I grabbed the nearest Bible within reach. It was a brand new leather bound *New Living Translation*, though at that time I did not see which translation I picked up. Mike had purchased it a week before at the Bible bookstore. My favorite Bible is the one from which I have preached since 1973; a good old *King James Version*. It was on my nightstand, but I was too distraught to walk to the bedroom.

I didn't look at the Bible translation I picked up, nor did I look at the book and verse. I simply slammed the Bible open and began to read aloud, drowning out every voice in my head, forcing myself to hear the words from **The Book of God.**

I read: *"He has made me grind my teeth on gravel. He has rolled me in the dust. Peace has been stripped away, and I have forgotten what prosperity is. I cry out, 'My splendor is gone! Everything I had hoped for from the LORD is lost!' The thought of my suffering and homelessness is bitter beyond words. I will never forget this awful time, as I grieve over my loss."* Lamentations 3:16-20 NLT.

As I read the words, and they began to take root in my heart, I said, "Lord, You're taking Mikey home, aren't You? I don't understand. But he's going to die, or You would not have led me to these Scriptures."

My shoulders seemed to fall to the ground under the weight of the knowledge. My heart broke into a million pieces. The tears that had run like a fountain just minutes before seemed frozen in place. I was speechless and motionless, numb with this revelation. My head bowed down with sorrow. There was no strength to speak, fight, or cry out in rebuttal.

It seemed that I sat in that comatose state for an eternity. Then the gentle voice of my Master spoke softly to my heart, *"Daughter, read on!"* I'm not sure where the strength came from to pick up the Bible again and begin reading aloud, but I obeyed and read the very next verse: ***"Yet I still dare to hope when I remember this***: *The unfailing love of the Lord never ends! By his mercies we have been kept from complete destruction. Great is his faithfulness; his mercies begin afresh each day. **I say to myself, 'The LORD is my inheritance; therefore, I will hope in him!'***

*"The LORD is wonderfully good to those who wait for him and seek him. **So it is good to wait quietly for salvation from the LORD**."* Lamentations 3:21-25 NLT

I spoke softly, hardly above a whisper, to the Lord. "Jesus, You are going to heal him in spite of the medical report. You are going to heal him!"

As I knelt there, I did what the scripture said to do. *Dare to hope* when you remember this. I could feel the Lord saying these things to me:

> "Remember: What I did *for* you at Calvary can be done *in* you."

> "That nothing is impossible with Me."

I could feel courage flowing into my soul's veins. As I reflected on His greatness, my sorrow was being washed away! The Lord continued,

> *"Remember that I raised the dead."*

> *"That I am God. Is there anything too hard for Me to do?"*

What we think matters. The situation had not changed. Mikey was still dying, but I had just heard from my Counselor, Friend, Healer, and Lord!

> *"Remember the many times I have delivered you."*

My mind was being renewed by the seconds in His presence. My thought pattern was changing. No more panic, hard breathing, uncontrolled sobbing—just the sweet calming presence of God strengthening, pouring in, renewing, restoring the volcano of my soul.

> *"You can dare to hope, DARE TO HOPE!!!!!!! Remember who I am!"*

Then I read the remainder: *"**So it is good to wait quietly for salvation from the Lord**."* Lamentations 3:26 NLT

I knew that God was going to heal Mikey. I didn't know when, or how far this would go; but I knew that I knew that I knew in my heart that he would live, and it would all be okay.

The weeks that followed brought some of the toughest challenges for my faith.

Bone marrow testing was one of the medical procedures given often to Mikey—and with no anesthesia. I sat in the room and listened to his pain. It was more than I could bear as a mother. I wanted to take the pain for him. I wanted his suffering to stop.

As the long dreadful days progressed, his bowels blocked, and his breathing became increasingly difficult due to the large growing mass in his chest.

One day, my emotions reeling, I just broke. I laid my head across his legs and sobbed saying, "Mikey, I am so sorry that you are going through cancer."

He sat up in bed and began to stroke my hair and said, "Mother, don't you know that my days were numbered when you conceived me and carried me in your womb, and until God is finished with me, I am immortal?"

Then he began to pray for me, "Dear Lord, give my mother and dad the same faith and peace that I have. Help them to trust You like I do." He continued his comforting caress of my head as he prayed, as if I was the one who was ill, instead of him.

Mikey continued to lose strength as the tumors kept growing. The last time they measured the large one in his chest, it was twenty-five inches long, seventeen inches wide, and seven inches thick. In the natural realm, things looked bad.

Very early one morning, I was in my home, deep in a prayer time for Mikey. We had house guests. Trying not to disturb them, I went into the den and covered my head with a blanket, trying to muffle the sound of my prayers. After much intercession, an indescribable peace flooded over my soul like a gentle flowing stream. As God's peace poured over my soul, I began to sing:

> *I care not today what tomorrow may bring;*
> *If shadow, sunshine or rain,*
> *For the Lord I know ruleth o'er everything,*
> *And all of my worry in vain.*
> *Living by faith in Jesus above.*
> *Trusting, confiding in His great love.*
> *From all harm safe In His sheltering arms.*
> *I'm living by faith and I feel no alarm.*[1]

It was at this moment that God spoke to me and said:

> *"From this day forth, Mikey will be breathing and living by faith. His very breath will come from me."*

Mike came to my little makeshift prayer tent and said, "It's time to go to the hospital, honey."

It was on that very morning, when God gave me this old hymn, and told me from that day forward

Mikey would be living by faith; it was that morning when Mikey refused any more chemotherapy.

Mikey's reason to refuse the barbaric treatment? He had overheard the nurse say he wouldn't be able to father a child if he took it. Because of this, the doctor declared he had only a twenty-percent chance of saving him.

Mikey continued to live, defying death. Mike and I discussed rescheduling our ministry time in Africa. We were scheduled to fly out in just a matter of days. Mikey overheard our conversation and said, "If you don't go, the devil will have won. You must go!"

So, go we did.

Not knowing—in the natural realm—if our son would live or die, it took complete trust in God. I had to believe what He had spoken to me from His Word in my living room weeks before when I had begged for His guidance. It was the only way that I could board a plane headed for the continent of Africa . . . so far away from our suffering son.

Mike and I walked up the ramp of the Northwest flight headed to Memphis and the regions beyond with our faces swollen from crying. Holding hands like kids, we leaned upon one another in unity, "If we are going, we will not go mourning and drowning in these tears. We will go in the joy of the Lord. We will go, believing for a miracle."

We agreed together, dried our faces—which obviously bore the deep pathos of our circumstances—squared our shoulders, and stepped inside the carrier to find our seats among the hundreds of travelers. It is in times like these that you can feel the very strength of God holding you up on the wings of His mercy and filling you with His power.

Thirty hours later, we arrived in Nairobi to the familiar choking smog of fumes from diesel engines which most Kenyan vehicles use. There are so many smells that assault the senses upon first arrival in this huge bustling city alive with frenetic activity. With open sewage or rotting garbage, the smell of diesel exhaust certainly is not the worst of them.

Arriving at Jomo Kenyatta International Airport late at night, we gathered our luggage and proceeded through the passport control. After seemingly an eternity, we cleared all the red tape and headed for the Utalii Hotel—a quaint modest hotel that is actually a training college for room stewards, cooks, and hotel personnel.

A dear friend, Bob Hoke, bought us a satellite phone so we could call and check on Mikey as often as we wanted, which was twice daily. It was before the days of the cellular phone madness in Kenya. Satellite was the only way to go. God bless Bob and Ruby for their thoughtfulness and friendship.

Everybody needs true friends; the ones that will stand with you during the hard times as well as the good times. As pastors, we have all experienced friends that will sail with you in your boat when the waters are beautiful and smooth. However, when turbulent waters start rolling in, we all have those fair weather friends who throw you overboard, leaving you to the sharks.

The only place to get a phone signal was the tiptop of the Utalii Hotel roof. The outside stairs went nearly to the top, and then a little ramp provided easy access to the rooftop. I made my way to the rooftop at least twice a day to call Mikey.

It wasn't easy to catch a signal. I really had to work at it. When I heard my son's voice, my heart leaped right out of my chest. "He's still alive! Oh, thank You, Jesus! You are so faithful!"

"How are you doing, son? Can you breathe? Can you walk?" The questions poured out too quickly for him to answer, but Mikey's answer was the same every time:

"Mom, I am blessed beyond the curse."

"Yes, son, I know that you are. But how are you really?"

"Mom, I'm blessed beyond the curse."

"Mikey, now listen, we are paying $5.00 a minute for me to know how you are doing. Please tell me the truth. Your daddy and I really need to know the truth, so now spill it. Talk to me."

"Mom, I'm blessed beyond the curse."

Frankly, I became upset. When I hung up, all I knew was that my son was *"blessed beyond the curse."*

Each day we repeated the same saga. But one day, it really hit my spirit what he was saying. Standing on the roof of the hotel, the light dawned in my heart like sun bursting forth on a clear morning, spreading colors across wispy clouds. *Mikey WAS blessed beyond the curse!*— the curse of cancer that had claimed so many of our family members too early in life!

During our devotions that day, God gave me a vision. I was worshiping him in the Holy Spirit, when I was slain in the Spirit of God. In the vision, I stood on a levee surrounding a field of a white-topped crop ready for harvest.

I had never seen this crop before—it was three years before I discovered it to be the yucca plant, also known as *Candle in the Desert*. Some of the stalks were straight and tall, while others were leaning toward the ground as if about to fall. Bonnie Ness, my friend and a long-time missionary to Kenya, was standing on my left, and my Saviour, Friend, Heavenly Lover of my soul was on my right.

"Bonnie, we need to harvest this crop while it is ready."

Bonnie replied, "What we *need to do* is to train harvesters to go out into the field for us."

At that very moment, one of the heads fell to the barren ground, and Jesus said with more emotion than I could ever explain, "Now that one is unsalvageable . . . forever. I need you to walk through the stickers and thorns, and salvage the others of the harvest before it is forever lost."

"Yes, Lord, I will go for You."

The next night, we began a crusade in a filthy area. Humans used the grounds for their toilet since none of the homes had indoor or outdoor plumbing. I sat on the steps of our vehicle complaining about the many goathead stickers stuck in my clothing. I murmured under my breath, saying things like, "I'll probably get AIDS from these filthy stickers. They really hurt my skin."

At that moment, God brought to mind my vision. I buried my face in my hands, wept, and repented of my selfishness.

"I'm going to live, Mom! I'm going to live!" Mikey spoke with all the enthusiasm that he had the strength to speak. "I awoke this morning with no pain. I called the doctor, and he said to come in for tests. When the tests were completed, the doctor told me, 'Well, son, you have your rare miracle. There is not a tumor or cancer cell in your body. Looks like you're going to live.' "

Within a week, Channel 10 News of Springfield, Missouri, interviewed Mikey as a modern day miracle.

I must add this conversation with my Lord: One day while in prayer, God told me that it was His plan to heal Mikey. If Mikey took medicine, He would use that. If Mikey took no medicine and trusted Him solely, that He would heal him that way, because it was His plan to heal Mikey from the beginning. Wow! God has a plan if we only *dare to hope*!

6
GOD'S ABSOLUTES FOR MIRACULOUS INTERVENTION

Dare To Hope

6

GOD'S ABSOLUTES FOR MIRACULOUS INTERVENTION

Dare To Hope

(Personal notes from the message birthed in this fiery trial of our faith.)

Lamentations 3:16-26 NLT,
He has made me grind my teeth on gravel. He has rolled me in the dust. Peace has been stripped away, and I have forgotten what prosperity is. I cry out, "My splendor is gone! Everything I had hoped for from the LORD is lost!" The thought of my suffering and homelessness is bitter beyond words. I will never forget this awful time, as I grieve over my loss.

Yet I still dare to hope when I remember this:

The unfailing love of the LORD never ends! By his mercies we have been kept from complete destruction. Great is his faithfulness; his mercies begin afresh each day. I say to myself, "The LORD is my inheritance; therefore, I will hope in him!"

145

The LORD is wonderfully good to those who wait for him and seek him. So it is good to wait quietly for salvation from the LORD.

What We Dwell On Really Does Matter!

Mikey said, "Doctor, are you threatening me with heaven? Heaven is no threat to me." He chose to dwell on the wonders of heaven, rather than the report of death and dying.

Proverbs 23:7 KJV tells us that *"as a man thinks in his heart, so is he."* Therefore, what we think makes a difference. You can't change your circumstances, but you can change your attitude toward your circumstances. This reminds me of the glass that is half full or half empty. The thing that most people fear is death. So, if death is no threat to us as believers, then why fear?

According to 2 Timothy 1:7 KJV, *"God has not given us the spirit of fear [this tells us that fear is a spirit] but of love, power and a sound mind."* This is God's promise to us, even in our darkest hour. He gives us a peace that passes human understanding, and a joy unspeakable and full of glory.

I dreaded seeing my son suffering with cancer, and felt sick at the thought of him dying. But once again, he put those feelings to flight when he said, "Mom, my days were numbered when you carried me in your womb. And until God is finished with me, I am immortal." This statement immediately refocused me on God's plan and not my fears.

The Word of God altered my thinking, thus altering my responses to the crisis. In other words, I can dare to hope when I remember the very nature of God, and when I remind myself of these key thoughts:

Nothing Takes God By Surprise.
Nothing Is Impossible With God.

God's Absolutes for Miraculous Intervention

What are the "Absolutes" of God?

1. With God all things are possible.

> Matthew 19:26 NIV,
> *Jesus looked at them and said, "With man this is impossible, but with God all things are possible."*

2. **Nothing is impossible with God.**

> Luke 1:37 NIV,
> *For nothing is impossible with God.*

3. **All things are possible to him who believes.**

> Mark 9:23 NKJV,
> *Jesus said to him, "If you can believe, all things are possible to him who believes."*

4. **Is there anything too hard for the Lord?**

> Genesis 18:14 KJV,
> *Is any thing too hard for the LORD? At the time appointed I will return unto thee, according to the time of life, and Sarah shall have a son.*

5. **I am the Lord, is there anything too hard for me?**

> Jeremiah 32:27 KJV,
> *Behold, I am the LORD, the God of all flesh: is there any thing too hard for me?*

6. **What is impossible with man is possible with God.**

Luke 18:27 NIV,
Jesus replied, "What is impossible with men is possible with God."

7. God can do all things.

Job 42:2 NIV,
I know that you can do all things.

8. ALL things are possible for God! Jesus said to His Father, *"Take this cup from me; nevertheless, not my will."* We must never forget that God has a master plan for our lives.

Mark 14:36 NKJV,
And He said, "Abba, Father, all things are possible for You. Take this cup away from Me; nevertheless, not what I will, but what You will."

9. God gives power to the faint.

Isaiah 40:28—41:1 KJV,
Hast thou not known? hast thou not heard, that the everlasting God, the LORD, the Creator of the ends of the earth, fainteth not,

neither is weary? there is no searching of his understanding. He giveth power to the faint; and to them that have no might he increaseth strength. Even the youths shall faint and be weary, and the young men shall utterly fall: But they that wait upon the LORD shall renew their strength; they shall mount up with wings as eagles; they shall run, and not be weary; and they shall walk, and not faint.

10. God gives us victory through our Lord Jesus Christ.

1 Corinthians 15:57 KJV,
But thanks be to God, which giveth us the victory through our Lord Jesus Christ.

11. Notice our victory comes through Jesus. In no way do we bring the victory.

1 Corinthians 15:58 KJV,
Therefore, my beloved brethren, be ye steadfast, unmovable, always abounding in the work of the Lord, forasmuch as ye know that your labour is not in vain in the Lord.

Help us, Lord, to be unshakable, unmovable, firm, fixed, and stable.

When I think of *steadfast*, I visualize a sentry guard whose feet are firmly planted—poised for battle, if need be. I think of a Maasai warrior who has placed his feet for battle against a charging lion. He stands his ground, even in the face of danger. The warrior is taught from childhood not be to a coward, not to run, but to be strong and unshakable. I have been told by Maasai men that if you shake, you cannot throw a spear straight.

Here is the difference: We stand firm—but the Lord fights our battles, and through Jesus Christ, we have the victory.

Let's be strong in the faith, confident in the resurrection, firm in our belief in the gospel, and unshaken by the battles of this life. As long as we live, we will face challenges. Only the dead have no battles.

Our battles do not destroy us. Rather it is the way that we respond to them. If we blame God, or drown in self-pity, we cannot hope to win. Nor can we rely on our own abilities. Our victories come through our Lord Jesus Christ!

Malachi 4:2-3 TLB,
But for you who fear my name, the Sun of Righteousness will rise with healing in his wings. And you will go free, leaping with joy like calves let out to pasture. Then you will

tread upon the wicked as ashes underfoot,"
says the Lord Almighty.

Don't be angry when trouble, sickness, hardships, or tests comes your way. The cares and temptations of life can be overwhelming in the land of the living. Don't listen to "Job's comforters" with worldly philosophy and lies that are directed at luring your soul into hell. Rather, focus on the Word of God, the power of the cross to save, the delivering power of the Almighty. And focus your binoculars upon eternity.

Focusing upon eternity brings a completely new interpretation to your circumstances and dealing with hard times. Jesus, the Author and Finisher of our faith, looked past the suffering of the cross to the joy that was set before Him. We must do the same. Look past your present trouble to the joy that awaits every believer. This is heaven!

Remember, we are not of this world. In it, yes. Just not of it. We represent a different kingdom, one not defined by riches, power, pleasures, or recognition. We are looking for a kingdom whose Builder and Maker is God. In our kingdom, we are taught to give, expecting nothing in return, to love the unlovable, and to forgive unconditionally. Our kingdom is contrary to this world's system of weights and balances.

Faith is a daring confidence that God will catch you when you jump.

We must know that our hope is not in vain, but it's for real. Hope is daring, alive, real, and it does make a difference!

> 1 John 5:4-7 KJV,
> *For whatsoever is born of God overcometh the world: and this is the victory that overcometh the world, even our faith. Who is he that overcometh the world, but he that believeth that Jesus is the Son of God? This is he that came by water and blood, even Jesus Christ; not by water only, but by water and blood. And it is the Spirit that beareth witness, because the Spirit is truth. For there are three that bear record in heaven, the Father, the Word, and the Holy Ghost: and these three are one.*

> 1 John 5:14-15 NASU,
> *This is the confidence which we have before Him, that, if we ask anything according to His will, He hears us. And if we know that He hears us in whatever we ask, we know that we have the requests which we have asked from Him.*

We must never forget that our Father knows what we need. We are sure of this one thing: that He always hears us when we pray. We are taught to ask, seek, and knock.

> Matthew 6:8 KJV,
> *For your Father knoweth what things ye have need of, before ye ask him.*

> Matthew 7:7-11 KJV,
> *Ask, and it shall be given you; seek, and ye shall find; knock, and it shall be opened unto you: For every one that asketh receiveth; and he that seeketh findeth; and to him that knocketh it shall be opened. Or what man is there of you, whom if his son ask bread, will he give him a stone? Or if he ask a fish, will he give him a serpent? If ye then, being evil, know how to give good gifts unto your children, how much more shall your Father which is in heaven give good things to them that ask him?*

Jesus confronted unbelief.

> John 6:26-27 TLB,
> *Jesus replied, "The truth of the matter is that you want to be with me because I fed you, not because you believe in me. But you shouldn't be so concerned about perishable things like food. No, spend your energy seeking the eternal life that I, the Messiah,*

*can give you. For God the Father has sent
me for this very purpose."*

Matthew 13:58 KJV,
*And he did not many mighty works there
because of their unbelief.*

Don't lose hope or faith in God. Remember that God causes us to triumph in Christ Jesus.

2 Corinthians 2:14 KJV,
*Now thanks be unto God, which always
causeth us to triumph in Christ, and maketh
manifest the savour of his knowledge by us
in every place.*

As Mikey so aptly spoke, "I am blessed beyond the curse."

You are blessed beyond the curse, rescued that you might triumph!

7
CATCH ME, DADDY, I'M GONNA JUMP!

Uganda

7

CATCH ME DADDY, I'M GONNA JUMP!

Uganda

"**G**et your house in order; you have eighteen months to live."

Perched on the end of the examining table, I felt jittery, like a caged canary with a cat prowling around outside. My legs swung nervously as I anticipated meeting the doctor for the first time.

"Just three more weeks and we leave for Africa," I had said with great excitement as we headed to the medical clinic just minutes before.

The year was 1985. My daughter Melissa, and Jean Rogers, a dear friend and sound tech, and I were gearing up for a concert tour in Uganda. When invited to the Dark Continent by the prime minister, I informed him in no uncertain terms that we would sing only gospel music. I added, "I'd like to give an invitation for prayer at the end of the concerts," and to my great surprise, he granted our wishes.

There was so much to do in preparation to leave, including a trip to the doctor for necessary shots to enter third world countries. This was definitely not my cup of tea.

Jean was kind enough to pick me up; actually, she is the one who made the appointment and then informed me about it on the way to the clinic. It had been years since I'd seen a doctor. I didn't even have one, nor did I want one. However, I needed all these silly shots, and I guess a little exam wouldn't hurt either, especially since I hadn't been feeling well for some time.

As I sat there anticipating the approach of the doctor, my mind was running in a hundred different directions: *"I'll bet he thinks I need to be on a diet. He'll probably tell me to start one immediately. Oh goodness, I forgot to shave my legs. What next! I wish he would just come and get this over. I wonder if doctors purposely leave you sitting, waiting, anticipating their coming so you will forget everything you wanted to ask, thus requiring another visit. I just want to get this exam over. I have too much to do to be here anyway. What a waste of my time. Uganda is going to be great. I can feel it!"*

"Hello, Mrs. Cheshier. Nice to meet you. What can I do for you today?" Dr. Cadeaux asked as he entered the room.

"Well . . ." I sounded tongue tied, like a giddy schoolgirl. Why do I act this way when I'm nervous? "Ah, well, I'm going to Uganda in three weeks, and I probably need some shots, and oh, yeah, I've been really tired lately. I'm sure it's nothing, but since I'm here. . . ."

Now that sounded stupid. Poor doctors have little to go on when I try telling them what's wrong with me. What is it about us non-medical folks? When we are in the presence of eight-plus years of an expert studying the human phenomenon, we develop either diarrhea of the mouth or constipation of the brain!

Without any trace of condescension, he began the exam.

"Let's just take a look," he said. He looked in my eyes, ears, nose, and continued to my neck. Then he pressed on my stomach. As he examined the breast, his light demeanor abruptly changed. He took on a concerned look and said, "I think you have a serious problem with your breast. It could be cancer. I want to send you across the street to a specialist right now. I'll have my nurse call his office and let them know you are on your way."

For a moment I was stunned speechless—a most uncommon place for me. What was he talking about? I didn't want to see another doctor. I didn't want to come to this one, and furthermore, I didn't have time for anything as serious as cancer!

Had I been alone, I would not have gone to the other office. But my faithful little friend walked me across the street to Dr. Demur's office. Jean is a colorful, peppy personality from French descent, about five foot, four inches tall with short brown hair. She escorted me as if we were going for my favorite ice cream sundae. No big deal! We'll scratch this off the list, and move on to the next item.

Dr. Demur, who was short, plump, and balding with dimples, put one in mind of the Pillsbury doughboy TV advertisement.

Without my knowledge, one of the doctor's office personnel had called Mike, who was studying at the church office in preparation for upcoming Sunday services. The nurse informed him that he needed to join me at Dr. Demur's office immediately. Mike was in complete confusion. He didn't even know that I was seeing a doctor in the first place. Why would I be in a surgeon's office? What could possibly be the reason for his needing to drop everything and join me? However, much to my chagrin, he did.

Dr. Demur tried unsuccessfully to draw fluid from the hard egg-sized mass in my breast. The lump had finger-like tentacles, which had caused the breast nipple to become inverted.

"Marigold, I'm sure this is cancer. We need to remove your breast ASAP."

"No, I'm not having breast removal. I'm leaving for Uganda in three weeks. There simply isn't time for this type of surgery."

I jumped off the exam table, put my blouse back on, and headed for the door so rapidly that one might question if a fire alarm had gone off. My mind and heart were racing, and I couldn't get out of there quickly enough.

Dr. Demur caught me in the doorway, put his plump arm around my trembling shoulder, and said, "We're going to be bosom buddies."

I couldn't help myself, I laughed out loud. At that very moment my husband, Mike, his face laced with concern and confusion came walking down the hall in my direction, escorted by the good doctor's nurse. The three of us returned to the exam room where Dr. Demur explained his concerns about my having breast cancer.

Mike's response totally surprised and angered me. He was ready to set the date and have my breast removed! I thought I might have a heart attack right on the spot from the shock of it all.

My face burned with anxiety, and I felt nauseous. "This can't be happening!" I protested loudly, feeling ganged up on by both guys. What do men know about losing your breast to some surgeon who has studied on unfeeling cadavers, and makes his living cutting open and stitching up patients while they are in an anesthetically induced coma, unable to protest? My breast is not just an appendage, guys!

I personally wanted no part of it.

"Marigold! When I married you, your body became mine, and if we need to have this surgery to save your life, then we will. It's as simple as that."

Easy for you to say! It's not your breast. Guys just don't get it.

"As I live, stand, and breathe, this body is attached to me, and I don't want this surgery, Mike. Please hear what I'm saying, I'm leaving for Africa in three weeks. This didn't take God by surprise. If I have this surgery, I won't have time to heal before I leave for Africa."

We continued to argue back and forth in front of the doctor, and occasionally he put in his two words. Mike continued pressing me to have the surgery, saying things like: "Your life is more important than keeping your breast. It's just an appendage," or "You want to be around to watch your children grow up." All of this made perfect sense to him as a man, but it left me feeling as if I was fighting a losing battle.

"Okay, okay, listen, guys. I'll tell you what I will do. You can remove the lump and no more. Leave my breast!! I don't have time to heal before I leave for Africa if you do such a radical surgery. But I will agree to have the lump removed to keep the peace in my home. And Doc, if you see that my breast is full of cancer, don't remove my breast, or I'll sue you." (I have never sued anybody in my life, and would never do so, but he didn't know that. By telling him this, I kept the upper hand—if there was such a thing.)

"You can only have the lump. I really mean this, Doc. Are we together on this?"

It was not vanity. If anything, it was cowardliness. But the truth was, I couldn't do this AND my missions assignment. Either I trust God in this— trust that this didn't take Him by surprise—or cancel my work and have major surgery. I just couldn't wrap my mind around the second choice. Call me cowardly, foolish, crazy, or vain if you wish.

Monday morning, bright and early, I was taken into surgery. The anesthesiologist gave me sodium pentothal, better known as the truth serum. Bad idea! Many people from the church where we served as senior pastors came to wait with Mike and to be among the first to hear the report after surgery.

Dr. Demur spoke as kindly as he could to Mike. "Marigold's pathology reports were not good. She has cancer. Every canal of the breast has a tumor in it, and each one is malignant. I'm sorry, Pastor. I did as she requested and only removed the one tumor, not her entire breast. Again, every canal in her breast has a tumor, and each one is malignant. It's important that we talk her into a radical mastectomy immediately! I believe the staff at MD Anderson Cancer Center in Houston, Texas would be able to convince her how life threatening it is to leave things as they are. I will make the call and get her in right now with your permission." Of course, he received no argument from Mike.

As I was rolled out of the recovery room, Mike met me and said, "My sweet sister Job." Hoping to give comfort, he chose the character he felt most typified the situation that I was going through. He was trying to be so tender and supportive. I, on the other hand, was full of sodium pentothal. This was not a good thing given my response to the drug known as "the truth serum."

"Don't you 'Sister Job' me! This is all your fault! If you had not made me have surgery, none of this would have happened!" (This was REALLY NOT a rational thought.) Of course, I don't remember saying any of this. Surely, it was the drug.

When I woke up several hours later, my dear daughter, Melissa, was tenderly running her fingers through my hair and comforting me. Through the fog of my drugs I asked her, "Where's your Daddy? Why isn't he here at a time like this?"

"Mom," smiling and speaking tenderly much like one would speak to a baby, she said, "you ran him and everyone out of the hospital—everyone except me, that is."

I didn't remember doing that. I felt so bad that I had done such a terrible thing! It sounded like I ran them out of the hospital like a drugged up hunter with a shotgun firing wildly at a covey of quail. I wonder what else I said "under the influence"? I don't think I want to know.

The next three weeks of preparation to leave for Uganda was anything but enjoyable. Through Mike and Demur's arm-twisting, I went to MD Anderson Cancer Center in Houston, Texas. After further testing, Dr. Fredrick Ames, the head of the breast cancer department, felt it important that we remove the breast immediately. However, just as before, I stubbornly refused. I knew that would cancel the ministry time in Uganda.

Had the time scheduled in Uganda not been scheduled, I have often wondered just how this story would be reading. Would I have had the courage to stand strong against all odds?

"You may not even live through your work in Uganda," Dr. Ames announced. "The cancer has been cut, causing it to grow."

Not knowing just how to respond, I said, "Well, ultimately it's my choice to live or die. I choose to trust God with the living and dying part of this problem. I promise that on the day after I return from Africa, I will come back to the hospital. You can check me." We made a deal, and I planned to keep my end of the bargain.

With fresh stitches in my breast, I felt as a poor steer must have felt in the Old West when a cowpoke held a red-hot branding iron to his backside. We three girls boarded a big metal bird heading east to Uganda with a layover in London. I must have melted into my seat, for I can hardly recall the actual flight.

A cheery voice broke into my painful rest. "Look around for your belongings as you disembark. It has been a pleasure having you fly with us today. Enjoy your stay in London."

I thought, *"Enjoy my stay in London? She's got to be kidding! I don't feel well, and certainly don't want to de-board this flight. My breast is throbbing with pain! What was I thinking trying to make this trip? I should be in a hospital somewhere, recovering from the surgery."*

"Lord, please help me."

Tears pooled in my eyes as I tried to gather the strength to collect my belongings. But instead, I just sat there, dreading the thought of trying to get up.

It's funny the things that God brings to your memory in times of trouble.

I glanced over at my beautiful 16-year-old daughter, Melissa. Normally, her perfectly proportioned slim figure is adorned with flowing auburn red hair. Light freckles add to her beauty, which has always been inside and out. However, for the occasion of our concerts, she had cut her beautiful hair into a darling short cut with blond highlights.

Instead, what I saw was a vibrant, enthusiastic two-year-old child playing in a churchyard where we were preaching a revival in Jonesboro, Louisiana. Mike and I were enjoying the sunny southern afternoon, allowing Melissa to run and play on the church grounds where we had our travel trailer parked for the week's ministry.

Because we were deep in conversation, Mike and I failed to notice that our adventuresome offspring, whose curiosity had gotten the best of her, had dropped back behind us. Melissa, having no sense of the danger, climbed a set of stairs on the outside of the building, which led to the rooftop of an old garage apartment. She leisurely walked across the rooftop to the edge of the two-story building.

"Daddy, catch me. I'm gonna jump!" With her little baby voice soaring with excitement, she leaped off the building.

Mike and I were in complete frantic shock when we heard her call out. Looking up to see where she was, we gasped.

Having played football in high school and college, Mike was quick on his feet and had fast reflexes. He dashed underneath Melissa and caught her in midair, kissed her on the cheek, and said, "Don't ever do that again."

As I prepared to leave the plane, I began my prayer, "Lord, I feel so exhausted. Please come to my rescue. I cry out to You today, the same as Melissa called out to us so many years ago. 'CATCH ME DADDY, I'M GONNA JUMP!' "

I felt strength begin to pour into my body from the top of my head to the soles of my feet, soothing me like warm oil, washing away the aches and pains within me. God had caught me!

His strength was made perfect in my hour of weakness. I actually felt like touring London town, and that is exactly what we girls did. We saw it all—Trafalgar Square, Tower of London, London Bridge, the Crown Jewels, Westminster Abbey, Buckingham Palace, changing of the guards—and then we ducked into a local pub for a pizza.

On a ride in a famous double-decker bus, my precious daughter chose to nap. However, I was like the Eveready bunny, energized by being in a place that I had never been before.

We toured for nearly the entire twelve-hour layover, and then boarded the big bird to take us to Nairobi, Kenya. From Nairobi we were scheduled to fly on to Kampala, Uganda.

As things tend to go in Africa, our flight to Kampala was delayed by a full day, causing us an overnight stay in Nairobi. Finally arriving in Uganda, we were delighted to see the small band of excited Africans waiting at the airport to greet us.

A spokesman said, "We were 300 strong yesterday to meet you. When you didn't show up, everyone decided that you had backed out of coming all together."

He continued, "We had an audience scheduled with the President. He wanted you to perform for him, and he was very disappointed. But, you may have been spared certain death, for a couple who had an appointment with him at the very same time you were to be there was shot and killed by a sniper at his parliament, right in front of him."

Prayers began to silently pour out of my heart. *"Thank You, Lord, for sparing our lives and looking out for us once again! I am so sorry that the couple was killed. But praise God, we weren't!"* Exactly what should I have said?

"Oh my, I was so upset that we were delayed. But now, I have to feel that our God was protecting us by delaying our flight. Please let the President know that these were circumstances beyond our control. We are so sorry about the couple that lost their lives. How tragic."

I didn't mention a revisit with the government leader, nor did he, for which I was thankful.

The sky, looking as if it had been gunshot, was turning blood red with a purple hue as evening approached. Our escort drove us through the large gates onto the Indian-red-earth courtyard of the Kampala guesthouse grounds. This area, which was African managed, was nestled on the side of one of the seven hills that surround the city of Kampala, Uganda, East Africa.

More than two dozen buzzards roosted along the eves and peaks of the roofs of one long slender building situated near a square one. Dogs greeted us by playing some sort of macabre game with several dead rats that lay by the entryway of what we soon learned was to be our sleeping quarters. My heart skipped a few beats as I scanned this dismal place. I could only imagine what my baby girl was imaging in her creative 16-year-old mind. The three of us looked at each other, speaking volumes without words.

Trying to appear enthusiastic, we entered our six-by-eight-foot room, furnished with three army cots to accommodate our sleeping needs. The space was so confining that it required stacking the cots on top of each other just to move around the room.

The curious lizards of all styles and colors, which inhabited the stucco walls, made us cringe. This was before the cute green gecko advertisements.

Night comes quickly in Africa. We barely managed to bring our luggage inside our cubicle before we found ourselves blanketed in darkness with no electricity to drive away the heavy blackness that an African night brings.

With divine help, we located our buried flashlights from deep inside our luggage. Not having been there long enough to familiarize ourselves with the grounds in daylight, we were unable to unpack. How I dreaded the thought of the remainder of our first night!

The warm May night, with its shadowy expanse over the smooth black air of the compound, made doodads crawl up and down my spine. With the beam of the flashlight, we could still see the pale shadows lurking on the roof. There was so much to process that I hardly gave thought to breast cancer, my decision to walk away from the medical help, or the political unrest I sensed in the very atmosphere.

We heard the deep resonant clangs of the dinner bell informing us dinner was being served. We giggled nervously, suggesting that maybe they were serving a little buzzard meat as an appetizer. The flashlights guided our steps to miss a few dead rats lying in the path. Yuck! Maybe it was rat stew instead. All the jesting did little for our appetite.

The few candles dimly lighting the dining hall caused us to hesitate long enough to allow our eyes to adjust to the darkness. It was certain that we wanted to avoid falling over each other or tumbling over anyone else venturing into our path.

We ate dinner, being the only wazungu (white folks) on the premises. Our table was fashioned from long roughly hewn untainted planks with crudely made benches to match. The meal consisted of thick porridge, flavored with meat unknown to our taste buds. That's actually saying a lot since we were all from Louisiana—we Louisianans have a reputation for eating anything that does not eat us first! We dared not ask about the meat. Somehow through it all, we had suddenly lost our appetite, so it really didn't matter.

Later that evening, I lay down on my cot and listened to the distant drums sending some rhythmic coded message. With the help of my little flashlight, I watched lizards scurry up and down the walls seeking food. The restful sleep my recovering body needed so badly eluded me. Try as I might to focus on the Word of God, all I seemed able to accomplish was scolding myself for dragging my daughter and friend to this dark, corrupt, dirty country.

My surgery site was throbbing with pain. The doctor's words, "Keep this bandage changed and the surgery site sterile," continued to replay in my mind. I realized there was nothing sterile about these sparse, dirty, rat-, lizard-, and buzzard-infested surroundings.

I began to stuff the many holes in the screen with a pack of moist towelettes to discourage mosquitoes from entering our sleeping quarters. I hoped to avoid malaria that was running rampant in Kampala, as well as most of Africa.

Only three weeks before I had been told, "You have cancer."

I had reluctantly agreed to the removal of the three-centimeter carcinoma tumor, but insisted on leaving the lubular carcinomas, which had invaded the inductral canals of my right breast. I opted to go to Africa and do the work of the Lord first. These reminders were ever looming just on the horizon of my mind. Slowly, my troubled spirit drifted into a few hours of disturbed sleep.

The next sound I heard was the singing and twittering of birds. I managed to crawl out of my cot, dress myself, and slip out of the room without waking the others. Standing on a hilltop in the cool African morning, I allowed the breeze and the smell of cook fires to drive away the night's cobwebs.

Weary, sore, and uncomfortable with our surroundings, I became angry with myself for accepting this invitation. I was lonely for the comfort of my strong husband's protective arms. I was worried about my son's care—he was only two and one-half years past his horrible, tragic burns. I was worried for Melissa's safety—she had been left for dead in a roadside park just months before, and was emotionally recovering from the terror.

I began to sob and call out to God for comfort. Actually, it was more like a wail. My bones ached. The very joints of my fingers agonized with pain. A cape of loneliness swirled and engulfed my very soul. I cried out, "God, I am such a fool. Why did I come? How could I have been so blind?"

The tears gushed from my eyes like a rushing current trying to burst through a forbidding rock wall. The emotions churning inside of my spirit begged for release, comfort, direction, and help. I simply could not hold back the fountain of tears.

Once again questioning, "Why did I feel I had to do this? Why did it seem so important? Why did I drag my beautiful daughter to this pit? My husband needs me. My son needs me. Oh God, help me now, or I'll die from a sickened heart. I can't stand this pain in my being another minute!"

Broken, I knelt in the red dirt, desperately needing God to help me. The Lord began to quiet my spirit, and my tears diminished. But my heart—that of a woman, wife, and mother—was still not at peace with the choices I had made.

I stood up, brushed the red dirt from my clothes, and prepared to go to church. It was Sunday, and we were the guest ministers. I had to pull myself together. The Africans would soon arrive to pick us up, and there was no turning back now. We had come to do a job for the Lord, and He would make us strong and able. I felt I needed to appear strong for Melissa. I simply couldn't allow her to see my pain; she must not watch me bleed. Though no one said it, I knew that it was hard for Melissa and Jean as well . . . but things were about to change.

We ministered in several churches that Sunday; however, it was the second one that made the difference for me.

When we drove up, we could hear over one-thousand people boisterously worshiping God inside the bamboo-walled and tin-roofed church. I made my way across the dirt floor and onto the rickety old makeshift platform.

While we praised God together, time seemed to stop. I glanced up to make sure that the roof was still in place, half expecting it to be lifted high in the air off the poorly constructed posts—all because of our praises to God. But, the only thing lifted was the gloom and despair that had earlier filled my heart.

Overwhelming joy flooded my spirit! Feeling like an eagle with oversized wings, I suddenly knew that we were on a mission from God, and were in the right place at the right time. The life threat of cancer had not kept us from this divine appointment. Now, at this moment, there was nowhere else on earth that I wanted to be except with this group of Ugandans, preaching the power and love of Jesus Christ.

It goes without saying that it would have been the better for my emotional state of mind had Mike and Mikey accompanied us on this adventure, but that had not been God's plan.

The first battle was won—the war that raged within the walls of my cranium.

Ours was the only vehicle on the grounds when we arrived at the National Theater. Our concerts were to start shortly—the real outreach ministry to the unchurched Ugandans for which we had traveled so far. Much to my surprise, when the concert began, all floors and all seats of the five-level theater were packed. People jammed into the corridors, stairwells, and aisles. Outside the theater, several hundred more fought to get in. Dignitaries, city councilmen, and leaders were among the audience, and I felt both blessed and overwhelmed.

While standing on the stage and scanning the audience, my mind drifted back to the hours that stretched into weeks of prayer. I sought to find the will of God—should I accept or decline the invitation for Melissa and me to hold musical concerts in the theaters and town halls all across Uganda? One particular afternoon while deep in prayer, my heart took off like a roller coaster.

Excitement and ecstasy welled up within me until I knew it was right for me to accept. At that very moment, the phone rang. The voice on the other end of the line was Daniel Satuka from Uganda.

He said, "Marigold, we must have your answer today."

"Hi Daniel, I'm coming. I'll be there, you can count on me," I answered.

A few minutes after I hung up the phone, I thought, "Oh, Lord! What have I done?" My carnal flesh feared the unknown, but my spirit knew I had reached the right decision.

During the next several weeks, I tarried before the Lord in prayer many nights until 2:00 a.m. and later. While deep in prayer early one morning, I felt the Lord impress me to provide 100,000 pieces of salvation literature and ten thousand Bibles as gifts to those who come forward for salvation during the concerts.

It's wonderful when a plan comes together!

With literature and Bibles in hand, we began the pseudo-concert tour across Uganda. I say this because, in the strictest sense of the word, they were revival services in which lives were changed and people were delivered from spiritual bondage. Each concert was three hours in length.

Alex Mukulu, one of our hosts who was an aspiring actor climbing the ladder of theatrical success, informed us that given the distance and difficult miles they walked in order to attend, if our concerts were shorter than three hours, the people might stone us.

Each day was an adventure with a variety of concert halls, city auditoriums, stadiums, and open fields being our venues. But one thing remained consistent: at the conclusion of every concert, the front filled with people responding to the call of salvation.

On one occasion, some Muslims stormed the auditorium and abducted the mayor who had just given us a huge cut out key. He had stated, "I am giving you the key to my city. I am so tired of killing and hate. I want my town to know this

Jesus that you are teaching and singing about. Here is the key to my city."

The attackers chain-locked the doors of the auditorium, and demanded that Jesus would not be preached in this city. I guess you could say that we were kicked out, the Word of God having caused a riot.

We went back to the guest house up country, and made plans to move on down the road the next morning. However, when our host Africans came to meet us they said, "Mama, we don't run. We will just move to the open stadium."

I thought, *"That's easy for you to say. You all blend together . . . sort of. But Melissa, Jean, and I stand out like a sore thumb. There is no missing our shiny white skin among a sea of black faces!"*

The next day we found ourselves standing in the middle of a soccer stadium, an open target for the angry Muslims. We sang, preached, and prayed in the name above all names—JESUS. And just like every other concert, hundreds flooded the open ground around us when we extended an invitation to accept Jesus as Lord. The mob pressed in hard enough that I climbed on top of the only table in the place—our PA system table— to keep from being trampled.

When it was all over, we loaded up the van with Bibles, literature, PA system, and fourteen passengers. Melissa sat by the front door; I sat beside her; next was Jean, and then the driver. We shifted from one hip cheek to the other. This was better than the space offered further back in the van. On the way, the driver stopped and bought a huge fish to take home to his family later in the week. He hung it on the windshield wipers—a real sight to behold—thankfully, most of the stink stayed outside!

Uganda has heavy vegetation, rich red soil, thick forests, and both two-legged guerillas and four-legged gorillas. Several times a day we were stopped at roadblocks and detained at gunpoint. The scary thing was the age of the gun bearers. They seemed far too young to understand the finality of death.

Refusing to look up, Melissa buried herself in an Agatha Christie mystery novel. That's like whistling a happy tune while walking past the graveyard. I tried to smile big enough to show all my white teeth, in hopes the young ones carrying machine guns on their shoulders would love the smile and choose not to shoot us. We had to show each of them the letter of invitation from the president and prime minister before they allowed us to continue our safari.

Much of the African adventure is centered on dealing with the local wildlife, while trying to minister. But Uganda was different. There was an evil bloodthirsty atmosphere, purely demonic, that saturated the air. At times, a million eyes could be seen staring at us in the night.

Sometimes the bedroom door would open; an evil presence would enter, then turn and leave. The eyes of the young gun-carrying soldiers were dark, empty, and bloodthirsty, just spoiling for a fight. The spiritual warfare was overt—in your face. Uganda, once the pearl of Africa, was now a pit of evil. But evil had to flee at the name of Jesus, and could not touch us!

The roads were so deplorable that the potholes had potholes! My stitches began to tear loose on the bumpy rides. All we had in the way of medical supplies were a few Band-Aid strips and scotch tape. My friend had insisted on bringing these things, and I told her that it was a waste of luggage space. Thankfully she hadn't listened. After we used all the strips, it was scotch tape until we arrived back in the States. That's what friends are for!

Melissa and I had a blast singing our mother-daughter duo concerts. Midway through our travels during a concert at a city named Jinja, Melissa touched my arm and I knew she had something important to share with the audience. I stepped back leaving her center stage and said a word of prayer for her. With many tears and unabated emotion, Melissa shared her testimony of the terrible assault, which had left her for dead in a roadside park just a few short months before this tour. Her story was real and it reached deep into the spirit of the war-torn, wounded people.

The Ugandans packed the altars, crying out to God for salvation, not realizing that within 24 hours, many of these who gave their hearts to the Lord would be tragically killed.

Just after we departed the next day to another town for yet another concert, guerrilla warfare broke out in Jinja, leaving hundreds dead in the streets, and closing all the roads exiting and entering the city.

We arrived in the town of Tororo, unaware of the tragedy of the bloodbath behind us. The Tororo Guest House, which boasted a grass or thatched roof where you could hear critters playing during the night, was the only accommodations available. We had to step down about twelve inches from the little wooden door opening to a hard-packed dirt floor. We could actually see through the open door slats where the owners had unsuccessfully tried to line them up. There was a small window with no screen or glass—just loosely-put-together wooden shutters. A bent nail was available to twist and secure the shutters closed. The beds were rickety cots with brown sheets—not from the dye, but from the dirt. The pillow was torn, exposing its inner parts with no pillowcase.

Melissa had no sleeping cap to protect her hair from creepy crawlies, so she created one out of her undies. However, the two leg openings left holes in her defenses. It took real *mind over matter* to lie down and try to rest.

When nature called, we faced an obstacle course. First, there was the step up and out onto a narrow walkway. We followed it to the open lobby where we stepped over people sleeping on the floor. From there, we continued out the back doorway and followed a dirt trail across the yard. Proceeding out the gate, and down another trail, we finally reached a wood-walled, dirt floor choo (rhymes with "toe").

There is a difference between an outhouse and a *choo*. An outhouse, also usually located down a trail away from the house, has some a resemblance to a sit-down toilet; while a *choo* is a hole in the floor that you stand over and trust you have very good aim. When Melissa was first introduced to the *choo*, she began to cry, saying, "I'm not going to go to the bathroom the rest of the time I am here." Realizing that was not possible, she continued, "I'll just go behind the bush with the other Africans," and that was precisely what she did.

We had lots of laughs—as on one occasion when I lost my underwear. I yelled to Jean for help when I got tangled up with pantyhose and my boots. Each and every visit to the *choo* was a balancing act, and we exited hot and stinky each time.

While in Tororo, Melissa ate undercooked eggs in an attempt to be courteous. She later paid the price for that act of kindness.

We entered the next town, and fearing we would have a repeat of the Tororo Guest House, I asked if there were any wazungu living in the area, Christian or not. I was directed to a compound just outside of town, to the home of an aging Canadian.

"Hodi," I called out at the gate. The elderly white woman came to answer my call. I described our reason for being in the area, and asked if I could pay her to allow us to stay with her tonight. I explained that I had an unsettling in my spirit about our wellbeing, and would be so appreciative if she would allow us to be guests, with pay, of course.

She flatly answered, "No."

I was stunned. She explained that she was angry, tired of the killing, scared, and packing to go back to Canada her home.

A heavyset lady walked to the gate from inside the house and said, "You can come with me. My husband and I are staying in an abandoned Methodist missionary compound. There are rooms that are shut off that we can open and clean. If you would want to stay with us, you are welcome."

Relief flooded my spirit, as tears pooled in my eyes. "May God bless you! Thank you so much!" I said, hardly able to contain my thankfulness.

Within six hours, Melissa was flat on her back with hepatitis. Her stools turned white, and urine turned brown. She was a very sick child.

We were informed that we could not return to Kampala the same way we had come because of the dead laying in the streets in the cities where we had been. War was breaking out all over the country, and within a few days, our lives were in greater danger than with the hepatitis or the cancer.

For the next few days, I sang alone.

The gracious couple with whom we lodged had come to Uganda to teach agriculture in hopes of helping the economy. They were not missionaries, but Methodist laypeople. On the third night of our stay, I asked everyone in the house to join us in intercessory prayer for Melissa. She was so sick, and I was terribly worried for her. They kindly accepted the invitation. We all knelt around her bed and earnestly began to pray. During the prayer time, our Methodist hosts, both husband and wife, were baptized in the Holy Spirit with the evidence of speaking in tongues. It was a glorious time. Melissa was healed and joined me in concert the next day!

"Mother, we must leave Uganda. God has spoken to my heart. You just love the people so much that you are not hearing God. But I am telling you, I know that I know that we have to leave this country!"

Not wanting a fight, I surrendered, and listened to my daughter's sincere belief that God had spoken to her. We cancelled the remaining week of concerts, and mapped a way to get back to Kampala in order to catch a flight back to Nairobi, Kenya.

Our last evening before leaving Uganda in the dust, turned out to be one of twisted excitement. I awakened from a sound sleep to the sounds of an Indian war dance wafting through the bedroom window. I immediately got up, looked outside, but saw nothing. I convinced myself the people to whom we had preached that day must have decided to have a late night service. No doubt, they were being filled with the Spirit of God, so I would just join them from the privacy of my bedroom. I raised my hands and began to praise the Lord.

The outside warlike whooping sounds increased, so I increased my inside praise. Soon I began to walk around my room, loudly praying in the Holy Spirit with hands raised. At times, I was so excited that I jumped for joy! Forget the cancer! Forget the sore stitches! I was having a great prayer meeting, praying in the Spirit, speaking fluently in a language I did not know.

The yelling from outside the window instantly returned to stark quiet. Assuming our prayer meeting was over, I returned to bed and went back to sleep. About 6:00 a.m., I spoke through my window to a young Ugandan girl that lived on the premises.

"Did you hear the prayer meeting last night? It was wonderful," I said.

"Mama, that was no prayer meeting," she replied. "That was a group of thieves who came to rob us. I found a place to hide, and don't know why they left without harming us."

H-h-h-h-um, I have a good idea as to why they left. They probably looked through the window and saw a crazy white lady with her hands raised high in the air, maybe even speaking their language telling them to get out! I had a hardy laugh at the very thought of the sight the astonished thieves witnessed. *"Thank You, sweet Jesus, for Your protection, even when we are unaware that we need protecting."*

We barely made it out of the country when Museveni overthrew Obote. It was a coup, a take-over, a blood-murderous war. One of the compounds where we were supposed to have stayed was taken at gunpoint, and all the women were brutally raped; some murdered. The Methodist couple, who had so kindly taken us in, escaped with their lives to hide in the jungle. All the while, the army burned, raped, and murdered anyone they could get their hands on, taking over all compounds. We would have been there had Melissa not heard from God.

Thank you, baby, for hearing the voice of the Lord!

After two months of ministry in Uganda, we safely arrived home, and may I say, "There's no place like home"? True to my word, in just two days, I made my way back to the hospital. I was excited to return to MD Anderson cancer institute in Houston, Texas so that all could see I was still alive and kicking. Cancer had NOT claimed my life.

I really felt in my heart that because I had put the work of the Lord first, there would be no trace of cancer remaining in my body. God rarely works as we tend to reason that He will. It would be nice if all our ducks lined up in a row, and life presented itself as a neat little package complete with a beautifully tied bow. However, as the Scripture says, *"His ways are not our ways and our thoughts are not His thoughts,"* but faith joins its voice with Abraham, and affirms that the Lord of all the earth shall do right.

At times, we feel brave and courageous, and other times like a terrified little puppy. When Melissa, my daughter, was going through a very tough time in her life, she often sang the song "The Warrior Is a Child." More times than I can count, I have felt like laying down my sword and falling into the arms of Jesus, weeping until there are no more tears left to shed. That childlike feeling can come unannounced, unexpected, and unwanted.

Having been a part of such a mighty move of God in Uganda, I began these unchartered waters of ill health feeling rather spunky in the faith. First of all, I did not expect an adverse report, but rather a positive one.

Life is made up of mountain peaks and valley experiences. I have often said only the dead have no challenges. As long as you wake up on the top side of the grass rather than the alternative, you will be faced with unpleasantness from time to time—like the night we were stranded, stuck in a ditch, surrounded by wild African animals, but that's another story yet to be written.

The husband of a family who had begun attending our church in my absence was scheduled for surgery in New Orleans at the same time that my surgery was scheduled in Houston. Mike, my husband, felt torn—should he stay with this new church member, or accompany me to Houston? I persuaded him that this man needed his attention, to pray for him and sit with his family during his operation, which is our custom as pastors and friends. Besides, his procedure was much more severe than mine. I would be fine by myself, especially since I was sure that I was cancer free. Usually in such dilemmas, my mother or my sister, Marcia, would step in to be with me; however, both were unavailable. Thinking we had no choice, Mike went to New Orleans and I went to Houston alone.

To avoid yet another scar in my breast that I had insisted on keeping, the doctors opened the same surgery site and removed the lymph nodes from my right side. I was in the hospital a week and in much pain—not just physical, but in my heart and spirit. Cancer was in the lymph nodes—not good since the lymph nodes are the filtering system for the body. The cancer had metastasized—spread to other parts of the body through the lymphatic system. Lying in the hospital bed in my room, staring at the walls while the drain in my breast and under my arm slowly caught the liquid oozing from of my body, I felt like an abandoned child. Knowing that it was the right thing for Mike to be with someone else didn't keep me from feeling lonely.

A battle of a different kind began to ensue, taking sides, swinging swords within my heart and mind. This war called resentment attaches itself to your heart like leeches sucking the life-giving blood from you. As believers, we don't like to put a name to this feeling because it sounds so un-Christlike and childish, but it took seed nonetheless. Poor Mike, caught in the middle! Although married to a preacher of the Word, and a faith-believing woman who was just that—a woman, I was blasted with feelings and emotions too hard for me to cope with. Tears flowed freely as I lay trapped by lines and IVs. Dark talons of depression dug deep into my spirit. Usually, I am a person who sees the cup "half full." As a case in point, I tend to excuse a waitress with an attitude by simply saying surely she must have been dumped by the love of her life or she would be happier. So these feelings were out of character for me. I told myself it was all right to feel all these emotions. After all, I had gone to Africa right out of the hospital, and the time there had been hard work, not recreational.

Daring to look past my female emotions, trying with everything in me to deny the inner pain, I told myself that Mike and I had made the right decision for me to go solo. Nevertheless, sometimes even when our minds know the truth, our hearts tells us a different story. How I longed for my husband's comfort and love to caress away my pain. I yearned for him to reassure me that everything was going to be all right. I craved his hand cradling mine. He would see to it that the nurses paid attention to me. But more than that, he would be the one holding the water for me to drink, and fluffing my pillow. I missed him. This became an open door for the enemy to enter and cause havoc within my spirit.

The only good thing that has come out of this part of the story is what we learned. Shortly after the man's surgery, the family moved away—no longer a part of our lives. Church members come and go, but the family will remain, therefore we must make each other top priority. From that point on, we have given first priority to each other. I suppose our children picked up this valuable lesson as well, for if there is any crisis, large or small, the entire gang shows up at the ER or wherever, whatever is happening. I really love that about our family.

A couple of weeks after the drain was removed and my body had time to recover, the doctors said I needed chemotherapy. I said no, and promptly walked out. We went to the hotel room where I paced back and forth arguing with God. *"I don't want chemo. I hate what it does to people."* God gently said to me, "What if this is My plan?"

"God, I don't like this plan." Again, gently God said, "What if this is My plan?" Finally, I knelt and surrendered my frustration to the Lord.

Early the next morning I went back to the hospital to see my doctor who was the head of the breast cancer department. Looking back on this story, it is amazing that he would see me without an appointment after I had so rudely walked out on him the day before, but he did.

I proceeded to tell him that I was against taking the chemo, but that for some unknown reason, I felt it was in God's plan. Wasting no time, the specialist stitched a line into my chest called a subclavian catheter. The chemotherapy would be administered directly into this line. A five regiment drug protocol was selected. The first drug was Adriamycin, better known by its nickname the "red devil." If this drug gets out of the line and onto the skin, it will eat through the skin worse than acid; it is wicked stuff. Tamoxifen, Cytoxan, and Prednisone were some of the others. Within two hours of my first dose, my hair began to fall out in large wads. I sat in a chair in my room, and Mike brushed my hair until I was completely bald. My nails came off. The tissue in my urinary tract, gums, and esophagus disappeared. I blotted my teeth clean with a sponge. The doctors had rarely witnessed such a violent reaction. I felt chemotherapy was barbaric treatment. The doctor said to me, "If everyone responded to this treatment like you, we couldn't administer it." My blood count dropped to 0.1.

While waiting for my blood count to rise to at least 1500, I returned home to the care of my local physician. He kindly sent his nurse to our home to take my blood count every day. He called my attending physician on one occasion at Anderson and said, "I have buried patients with a higher blood count than Marigold's. You're killing my patient."

Weeks went by, and my blood count didn't come up high enough for another full round of drugs. Rather than driving back to Houston for this second treatment, I went to a hospital in New Orleans to a doctor who had previously worked at MD Anderson and agreed to work in co-operation with Houston. The physicians felt my system could not tolerate a second round of treatment, so they dropped all the drugs except for the "red devil," but only gave me twenty-five-percent of it. My body chemistry did not tolerate this either.

My brain throbbed as a caged prisoner trying to escape through the bars constricting its release. I held my head in my hands, and imagined the relief if it were immediately cut off.

Back into the hospital I went. When the doctor examined me, he muttered a few curse words, slung his clipboard onto the shiny floor, sending it sailing to the other side of the room where it landed with a protesting crash. Exasperated he said, "You have spinal meningitis."

For me, the bottom line was more needles, probing, and pain. At this juncture in my wrangling with cancer, rather than developing a tolerance for shots and IVs, I had a ripening phobia of needles, and a very low tolerance for pain and sickness in general, wanting no part of it. To this day when I see a nurse headed my way with a shot for me, my hands start sweating and I feel my heart fluttering. When it comes to medicine, I am truly a chicken-hearted, lily-livered coward.

A spinal tap was administered—an agonizing experience, I might add—which ruled out meningitis. I think that is a *"Praise the Lord."* The next step was an MRI to rule out breast cancer metastasized to the brain. Having no clue as to what an MRI entailed, I was in for a big surprise. *"Think about it, Marigold,"* I thought, *"what can a harmless machine do to hurt you?"* Naiveté can be fool's paradise. The MRI proved to be the most difficult test of all.

I am blessed, or cursed, with allergies of all kinds, especially to drugs. I could never be a drug addict. They gave me Valium to calm me down for the test, and it did just the contrary—I was bouncing off the walls. They gave me Demerol—I hallucinated and saw rats attacking, bees by the hundreds stinging me, and regurgitated. The sullen technicians sent me back to my room like a child being punished for misbehaving in class, and rescheduled my test for the next morning. *"Lots of luck with that,"* I thought.

With a massive headache that had now lasted for weeks and was apparently unstoppable, short of my extermination, I knelt in the bathroom floor with my head drooped into the shower, praying that God would help me make it through this test from hell.

When morning finally dawned, an orderly appeared in the doorway with the wheelchair, ready to escort me to my newest torture chamber—fondly dubbed "The Tomb" I am sure by those who never had the test, but an appropriate name if you ask me.

Despite my all-night prayer meeting attended by me, myself, and I, and the Father, Son, and the Holy Spirit, I was nervous as a cat on a hot tin roof. I lay on the constricted slab as they began the ritual of harnessing. The nightmare began. My pulse escalated. I heard my blood rushing in my veins, wanting to take leave of this body and find another. The cells screamed, *"What! This again! How could you?"* *"Come on, guys, we can do this,"* I told myself. A baseball-like helmet was locked into place across my face. I silently prayed, *"Jesus help me do this."* My ankles were strapped down, causing my leg muscles to twitch at the thought of not being able to move. Then came the wrist straps. No longer were my hands free to protect me. I was completely, helplessly constrained. All that was missing was the straightjacket. In spite of my self-talk, my mind whirled. I couldn't take a deep breath, making me think asphyxiation would surely be my demise. My heart knocked at my chest wall. Fainting or blacking out would be a welcome relief.

Terrible apprehension crowded my mind as the technician punched the button launching me through the horror inducing dark tunnel, at the speed of an African caterpillar, which increasingly aided the anxiety. The coffin swallowed me gradually. A *freaking out* state of mind descended upon me. My headache was so intense that I thought my skull might shatter. *"I just can't do it! I don't care what is wrong with my brain. Get me out!"* The words began in my mind and then at some point went audible. "Get me out!" I begged, "I can't stand it!" I shrieked as I pleaded like an animal begs for release from slaughter. I heard their protest to my request.

After seemingly an eternity, they reluctantly punched the button that started the tortoise like shift out of the burial vault. The frustrated technicians said, "One way or another, we have to get this MRI." Thunderstruck, I sat in the chair, unwilling to be constrained one second longer, refusing to even look *at the elephant* in the room. Short of taking a hammer to my head and knocking me out cold, I could think of no course of action.

Mike, my hero, spoke up with a proposition. "If this test is that critical, then you must allow me to go into the machine with Marigold." The technicians exchanged glances, flashed a look my way, and actually consented to his outrageous game plan.

After I was belted and padlocked down Mike laid his face on my legs and stretched out his body on the remainder of the mobile gurney and into the dungeon like capsule we were slowly propelled. Mike gently said, "Marigold, don't open your eyes. I am with you." Then he began to quote Scripture. With each spoken word my heart calmed. "Darling, keep your eyes shut; it won't be much longer." His words were soothing. He sang to me wonderful songs filled with comforting words about our sweet Lord Jesus. His sweet voice brought solace to my troubled soul. Warmth from his presence radiated through me.

"Don't open your eyes; you only have five more minutes." He declared his love for me, and I drank it in like one parched and dying of thirst, willing myself to obey his request not to open my eyes. I trusted Mike to lead me through the gloomy waters. His voice had quieted the anxiety in my spirit. For me, that day, he was Jesus with skin.

"Just two more minutes. It's almost over, sweetheart. You've done it, baby, you're through." *"No, Mike, we've done it,"* I thought, and I couldn't have succeeded alone. I felt the bed began to slowly exit the dungeon. Soon the light from the room began to peep out from under the end of the tube much like a morning sun rising, driving out the dark shadows of the night. First at my knees, then the waist, chest, and, o-o-oh-h yes, my face. Thank You, Jesus, and thank you, Mike, my love, my hero, knight in shining armor. The 45-minute unnerving test was now behind me because my sweetheart was willing to go far beyond the norm to rescue me.

The MRI revealed a pseudo brain tumor. In the words of the doctor, it was the size of my brain and half its size again, and it was oozing down my spine.

Because my blood count was dangerously low, I was warned to refrain from public places. I went to church and took a somewhat isolated seat on the platform. I wanted to worship God with my friends. Each time we gathered together the Spirit of the Lord renewed my mind and restored my heart. It was a wonderfully refreshing respite from my dreary fight against cancer.

This Sunday would prove to be like none other. I could hardly wait for the last person to exit the altar area so I might kneel and pray. God's presence was so real. As I prayed, I didn't ask to be healed or for the pain to stop. I was hungry and thirsty for something of much greater value; I wanted more of Him. I cried out, "Lord, don't take Your presence from me." Unaware that the church was now empty, time melted away.

I was seated in a heavenly place around a large campfire. Also present in this gathering encircling the fire were Abraham, Isaac, Jacob, Shadrach, Abednego, Meshach, Joseph, and many more great men of God. As far as the eye could see, angels were dressed in white with their mouth slightly open in an expression of awe hanging on to every word that was spoken. Those great warriors of the faith one-by-one told their story of how they had overcome the wicked one in the land of the living.

When one of the three Hebrews began to give an account of their bout with Nebuchadnezzar and the fiery furnace, I jumped up and said, "I've heard your story. All of us who read and love the Word of God know it, but you have not heard mine. May I tell of how God delivered our son who was burned from his waist up including his face? He died five times, and God brought him back each time."

I told the story in full detail while everyone listened. Their expressions let me know they completely understood the battles. When I completed Mikey's story, I told about Melissa and her life-threatening attack by murderous men who left her for dead in a roadside park. I related how God had restored what Satan had stolen from her. No one was in a rush: everyone was rejoicing over the victories, and the angels were mesmerized. The gathering seemed to say, *"Keep going, and tell us more."*

I started relating my fight against cancer and all the near-death experiences. It suddenly occurred to me that I did not remember dying. How did I get here? Did I miss my own funeral? I became aware of a Presence standing beside me. I could not look into His face. Everyone knew that He was there, and all were lovingly comfortable with such Royalty being present.

He gently took me by the arm and led me away from the group. We walked together down the most beautiful path lined with brilliant green shrubs dripping with a honey-like substance from every leaf and limb. Jesus said, "This represents My love covering every part of you—thick and protective, bathing and sheltering from the atmosphere around you." I understood what He was saying.

We came to a room to my left. It was like no room I had ever seen before. It was made of a cloud-like substance, guarded by several angelic beings with drawn swords. They indicated that I was not allowed to enter. Jesus spoke to them to let me pass through. I took one step inside, but the glory was so bright that I quickly stepped back beside the Lord. I was the one not ready to enter. He did not scold me, but rather took me by the hand, and together we walked further down the path.

We came to a room like any normal room. People I knew were in that room, but they were unaware of my presence. I saw the story of an attack against me unfold, but it had no effect because the Lord stood by me. It was just information. We continued down the path, and God showed me a second normal room with a different person in my life holding a knife in her hands ready to take purpose in my back. This, too, had no effect on me. We continued our journey to yet a third room. Again, the Lord showed me a scene that would come to pass in my life. Once again, I felt no pain of betrayal, only the knowledge that this would one day take place, God knew all about it, and would be with me every step of the way.

As we came to the end of our walk, I began to wake up. I was stretched out on the floor of our church halfway under the front pew. Mike was leaning over me, uttering, "Marigold, are you okay? Honey, can you hear me? Marigold, wake up! Marigold, Marigold."

I opened my eyes, slightly surprised not to be in heaven. I tried to answer, but spoke in a language we did not know. For a good half hour, I could only speak in a heavenly tongue. When the English words finally came I said, "Mike, when we get to heaven, we have a story to tell, and the angels will listen as we tell our stories of how we have overcome the wicked one in the land of the living. We must respond with faith in God to every situation. We will tell our stories in heaven, and if we are faithless or accuse God, then we will bring shame to ourselves." I repeated this over and over to Mike as he continued to get me to my feet.

Although completely bald, with grey-toned skin, and sickly thin, I felt like a healthy lioness ready to take on the world. I saw everything from a different perspective. Since then, as things come my way, I ask myself, *"Will I be proud of this response when I tell my stories in heaven? Can I relate this, or is this faithless and shameful?"*

Eventually over the course of many years, the events God allowed me to see during my visit to heaven have taken place just as I witnessed them. I've never handled rejection well; however, these three incidents only made me feel sorry for the perpetrators because I had been pre-warned by God and knew that one day they would take place.

Over the course of that year, I was hospitalized eleven times. While enduring much pain and weakness on one occasion, I began to come to grips with the fact I was dying, and that was that. I had been unable to eat anything in over a week. Yet another tube fed me. The lining in my mouth was completely gone; and even if I could swallow, nothing would stay down. I could see the handwriting on the wall—my time on earth was over, my heart was clean before the Lord, and I was ready to go home to be with Jesus. The thoughts of Mike, my precious Mikey, and Melissa carrying on without me pulled at my heart. If my time had come—and it seemed it had—I was willing to surrender to my dear Saviour who knew right where I was. Had I really thought it through, there were three incidents yet to come my way that God had revealed to me in my vision. My time to die had not come, but my body said differently, and I was too tired to fight any more.

You could hear a pin drop in my hospital room when Mike walked in the next day. The atmosphere was peaceful and serene. He said, "Marigold, what's wrong? You're way too quiet."

For a long time I said nothing, then in blunt soft tones I said, "Well, I guess I'm going to die. I've thought about it during the night, and Sarah (fictitious name) would make a great mom for the children and a good wife to you." I let the words hang in the air without further comment. For what seemed an eternity, Mike sat there stunned at my candid straightforwardness. He had always known me to be a person of faith. I am fond of quoting, "A positive mind is a powerful tool in the hands of a supernatural God." To give in was out of character for me.

Mike's neck gradually began to turn crimson, rising up his body like a thermometer submerged into hot water. When it reached his face, he exploded from his chair like a man stung by a hornet; came to the bed—a man on a mission; placed his knee on the bed for leverage; and grabbed the neck of my nightgown, pulling me nose to nose to him. He yelled in my face like a military sergeant calling his troops to attention.

"I'm getting no sympathy here," I thought.

"No, you're, not! God wouldn't do this to me. You're not going to leave me with these two heathens to raise alone. Fight! Marigold! Fight! Do you hear me? Jesus took this stupid cancer to the cross 2,000 years ago so you don't have to! Now you fight!" His voice matched his red countenance. He was angry at me for giving up, and terrified at the thought of being left alone.

I thought, *"He's gonna kill me if I don't do something."* So I picked up the control and buzzed the nurse. I said, "Bring me food; I'm gonna live." I wanted to show Mike that I was fighting.

The nurse came into the room and informed me that I was being fed through a line and couldn't swallow food. I informed her that if she didn't bring me food to eat, this husband of mine was going to kill me.

"Well, we can't have that," she said. She exited the room, then returned with a bottle of Lidocaine. "Drink this, and with a little bit of luck you will be able to eat." I drank the disgusting liquid, ate soft food, and promptly hurled. The nurse looked at me as if to say, *"See I told you so."*

"Bring more food, please." Once again, I drank the sauce to numb the esophagus, and tried again. Just as before, I threw up everything undigested. This continued about three days. However, little by little, I began to retain small amounts of soft food. It didn't take long to regain my strength. Praise God for a stubborn husband who wouldn't allow me to give up. After some time, I was able to return home.

Back to church I went, and of course wanted to give a testimony, which went something like this. "I want to thank God that He trusted me and my family not to blame Him foolishly for all the fiery furnace trials that have come against us. God could have kept these things from happening, but for some reason, He has allowed it. Just maybe the devil said, 'If You will let me hurt them, they will no longer brag on You so loudly, but will accuse You for not being their Protector. Maybe they will even say that You did this.' "

" 'Maybe, just maybe,' God said, 'they love Me and know I would never do such a thing. They will love Me and serve Me regardless. You can go this far and no further.'

"Just maybe God trusted us to love Him no matter what. Regardless of the reason, I feel honored to be trusted by God not to let this come between our love relationship."

I thought this made perfect sense. I could see it so clearly. I learned on that Sunday that some things should not be shared publicly. The carnal mind cannot receive the spiritual. Two families left the church never to return, saying they had never heard of anything so bizarre and sick-minded in their lives.

The cancer saga continued. Chemo had to be stopped after the second twenty-five percent dose due to my drug allergies and the fact that it nearly killed me.

I was back in the hospital once again for what would turn out to be my final visit because God was calling my name for a miracle. I think as you hear this part of the story, you might agree that He could have said, "I'll show you."

My roommate, a woman younger than me also with breast cancer, began moaning during the night. I lay listening and quietly praying for her to find relief; she did about 7:00 a.m. as she breathed her last breath. At 9:00 a.m. she was discovered deceased when her husband came in for a visit.

Shortly afterward, when Mike came in see me, I relayed the night's happenings. I'm not sure if it was fear of losing me or an explosion of faith, but he took my hands and prayed the doctor would come in and send me home.

Within five minutes the doctor walked into my room, sat on the side of my bed, and with an attitude said, "When we could have helped, you had to go to Africa and preach. Now we are sending you home with medicine to make you comfortable until you die. We think you have about eighteen months at the most.

'You are like that dumb Cajun who was caught in his home during a flood. He prayed that God would save him. The rescue unit came by in a boat and said, 'Get in and we'll take you to safety;' but he said, 'No, God will save me.' After a couple of hours, the water still rising, he was forced to sit on the rooftop of his home. The same rescue unit came to him and said, 'Hurry, get in, and we will take you to safety.' He replied, 'No, God will save me.' Later, he was sitting on top of his chimney and the third boat came. The driver said, 'Get in, man; we'll take you to safety.' The old Cajun replied, 'No, God will save me,' and he drowned. When he got to heaven, he said, 'God, why didn't You save me?' and God replied, 'I sent three boats, you fool.'

"Marigold, you were a fool to go to Africa when we could have saved you. I'm sending you home, as there is nothing else that we can do medically. You have eighteen months at most to live, so get your house in order. I'll give you pain medicine and help in any way that I can. I'm sorry. You should have let us save you when we had the chance, but no you had to go to Africa."

We said, "Praise God, hallelujah!" and I added, "I like that."

The doctor said, "Did you hear what I just said? You are dying."

Mike said, "Doctor, we just prayed that if God has healed Marigold, you would come into this room and send her home. You're not sending her home to die; you have just released God's hands to heal her." This made the doctor angry. We later learned that he is a Jew, and greatly resented us giving Jesus the credit for saving and healing.

He picked up the phone and called the x-ray department. He said, "I'll prove to you that you are still dying." He spoke into the phone, "I want x-rays and scans of Marigold." Shortly they came with a wheelchair to take me to the x-ray department. I wanted to say, *"Don't you know that x-rays can give you cancer?"* But I refrained.

They ran several different tests and found nothing. The doctor said, "Be back in three weeks; cancer doesn't just disappear." In three weeks, I went back for more x-rays. I did this many times until he said come back in three months.

When I returned, I had black curly hair and looked like a picture of health. He insisted I must still have cancer, but the technicians just couldn't find it.

I placed my hands on my hips, sashayed a little twist, and said, "Now, doc, do I look like I'm dying?"

He replied, "You look disgustingly healthy." We both chuckled.

My breast doctor at MD Anderson wrote a letter to my insurance company stating they should not hesitate to give me coverage. He said, "Concerning the cancer, we did not cut it out nor cure it, and it is gone. We believe a higher power intervened in Mrs. Cheshier's life, and we don't expect to see the cancer return again."

I am healed, truly healed, and it is documented because I dared to follow God's plan.

HEALED OF CANCER

Marigold

In 1985 Marigold was diagnosed with cancer and given 18 months to live. Now 12 years later her story is a testimony of the power of God to heal today.

The doctors stated, "We did not cut it out, we did not cure it with medicine, a higher power than us did the work." In Acts 4: 7 of the Bible, Peter and John were asked this same question after a lame man had been healed; "By what power or by what name has this been done?" Their reply was the same as Marigold's to her doctors and everyone that asks- Acts 4:10- "...By the name of Jesus Christ of Nazareth."

Today Marigold stands before you completely healed of all cancer.

Psalm 102:18 KJV,
"This will be written for the generation to come, that a people yet to be created may praise the Lord."

The following year, after my battle with cancer was concluded, Mike, Melissa, and I returned to Uganda for ministry. The Ugandans had hung banners stretched across the highways announcing our crusades and concerts as *The Marigolds*, which didn't make my daughter, Melissa, very happy. She was quite upset, but had no choice but to flow with it. You can only imagine how Mike felt. I thought it was hilariously funny.

The saddest part of our return trip was when we viewed the carnage from the war we had barely escaped. Our hearts felt crushed when some Christians took us to visit caves, buildings, and rooms filled with the hundreds of skulls revealing bullets to the brain as the cause of death. These were the remains of the martyred, left as a reminder of the political takeover that had taken place on that dreadful day one year before. No doubt, some who had attended our concerts were among the dead.

Many times during my life, whether it has been a fight with cancer or some other difficult situation, I have found God to be my Refuge. At times there seems to be no way out of arduous circumstances. Perched at the edge of a cliff, with wolves howling behind me, I have more than one time said, "Catch me, Daddy, I'm gonna jump!"

Faith is a daring confidence in God to catch you when you jump. He is worthy of our complete trust.

I feel sure if I live long enough that I will once again come to a place of reckless abandonment, relinquishing my own understanding to His divine wisdom, trusting Him to do what His Word says He will do. *"CATCH ME DADDY, I'M GONNA JUMP!"*

8
TEN COMMANDMENTS
OF FAITH

What Is Faith?

8

TEN COMMANDMENTS OF FAITH

What Is faith?

Many times I have been asked the question: "What is faith?"

The Ten Commandments of Faith that follows these two stories is a great guide in our quest to obtain true faith. Trust and simple obedience to the Holy Spirit that lives within every believer is also faith.

BACK FROM THE DEAD

I was making preparations for an upcoming ladies' meeting in Sandusky, Ohio that was yet a week away. While seeking God for His direction concerning what He would have me share with the ladies at the meeting, I felt compelled to fast. I did not know how long the fast would last, just that I was to pray and just drink water for my substance. When I call myself to a fast, I'm famished the whole time; but when God calls me to a fast, I don't suffer with hunger pains. Try as I might, I couldn't figure out the reason for this sacred time of prayer. My family seemed to be doing great, the church where we pastored was growing, and none of us was fighting a dreaded disease. Obedience is a key factor in our relationship with God. We don't need to be *in the know* as to *why* the Spirit of God compels us to do something we were not expecting; we just need to obey.

The day of my meeting fell on the seventh day of my fast. I felt strong in the Lord as the services began. There were eleven churches gathered together for the special Saturday service. As the guest speaker, I was seated on the platform. The sanctuary was full with the overflow attendance seated in the balcony along with a video camera. The pastors of the participating churches had remained in the service rather than leaving it with the lady folk. The director opened with a few songs, and turned the service over to me.

I was sitting there thinking, *"This service is so dead. No one is excited about what they are singing. What can I do to get these ladies on their feet praising God?"* I decided not to introduce my song or even say hello. I thought, *"I'll just start singing a high-energy song of praise, and surely they will join in."*

I graciously accepted the cordless microphone and began to sing as if there were thousands in the audience praising God with great joy. I began the peppy song with energized animation, presenting it lively and vivaciously.

> *David was a man of praise,*
> *praising God in the sanctuary.*
> *He praised Him on the trumpet and harp,*
> *and he praised Him in the dance.*
> *Now I don't want to offend anybody,*
> *but I came to worship Jesus,*
> *And if I hold my peace*
> *the rocks are gonna cry out.*[2]

This song is very upbeat. I call it a leg-slapping, foot-stomping, and hand-clapping song. However, no one, and I mean no one, was slapping, stomping, or clapping. Rather, they were looking at me as if to ask, *"What rock did she crawl out from under?"* It didn't take a rocket scientist to clearly see that I was the only one dancing and praising. At a time like this, the speaker has a choice. You can select a hymn to sing next; forget singing altogether and preach a message on the joy of the Lord; or close your eyes and don't look at their faces and keep on praising, dancing, and glorifying God. I chose the latter, much to my later chagrin. My song continued:

Well, there is one less stone
and one more voice
That's gonna praise the mighty name,
The name of my Lord.
There's one less stone and one more voice
To praise Him.
Blessed is the King Who comes in the
name of the Lord.[2]

While singing the chorus, I walked off the platform into the crowd of ladies to try and encourage them to praise God with me, raise their hands, or clap with the music. Maybe if we're up close and personal with each other, they would lose this stark fear, get their eyes off me, and began to praise the Lord.

Approaching my last note, I was faced with another decision. Should I just hold the note out, thus ending this song melodramatically, or should I do a nice jazzy run and give it a dynamic ending? Once again, I chose the latter. I closed my eyes and *let it rip*—musically that is. This simply put translates into *"you give it all the gusto that you have!"* When the music ended, I opened my eyes and found a lady, dropped dead, right in the service. Yes, you heard me right, *dropped dead*. As in gone, not breathing. Dead! My music had killed her for sure! Now I knew why God had called me to a fast. It was to strengthen me to make it through this humiliatingly, dreadful episode.

The director stepped over and took my microphone announcing that it looked like this retired missionary had died. She continued, "While doctors are on the way, wait quietly in prayer." Everyone was in shock. So was I! She was loved dearly. Her husband had graduated to heaven five years before, and now they were together.

My mind was swirling in a hundred different thought patterns as I sat on the platform. *"I can't believe this. God, why did You let this happen? If it was her time to go, You could have waited until the service was over to take her home to join her husband on the hills of glory. Did she have to go right now? At this very moment?"*

Then another thought came to mind. *"No one will book me as a speaker if people start dropping dead when I sing. How could you let this happen? I can read the advertisement now!"*

The twenty minutes that it took the paramedics to get there seemed like an eternity. Her body was stretched out on the foyer floor. Two doctors and two nurses attended to her. Word was sent to the director that she indeed was dead and had died of a massive heart attack. The director gave the grim announcement, and more tears were shed.

I was not ready for what transpired next. To my astonishment, she turned and handed the microphone to me as if she didn't know what else to do with it or with the ladies assembled there. Why didn't we just dismiss? What was I to do? It wasn't my place to dismiss. Funny thing about Bible School—we were never taught how to handle such matters. Have you ever played "Hot Potato"? It's a game in which you pretend that the object passed to you is too hot to touch, so you quickly pass it on. I suddenly wanted to pretend this microphone was a hot potato and toss it before my hand had time to cradle it. I stood speechless before these ladies. I had never even greeted them. I had only sung my murderous song.

I prayed, *"God, what do I do now? I can't just preach or say turn to page 100 in the hymnbook and let's sing 'Shall We Gather at the River.' Lord, I need direction. I can't greet them now. It's too late."* Running through my options, I found only one. I waited before the Lord, earnestly seeking His divine direction.

God spoke to me, *"Go pray for her."*

"Father, are You serious? No, I can't do that. They already think I'm crazy. If I go pray for her now that she has been pronounced dead, it will confirm that I am crazy."

Clearly, God spoke to me again, *"Go pray for her!"*

"Father," I argued, *"there are eleven men pastors here. If You want someone to go pray for her, ask one of them. They are men: it will be more proper."* No one moved. The whole place was frozen in place! No one was doing anything.

Again I heard the voice of the Lord say, *"Go pray for her."* Obedience is one of the toughest things you will ever do, especially when you know you are going to look foolish.

The word *obedience* reminds me of a story I once heard about a German Shepherd that was enrolled in obedience school in an effort to tame his independent spirit. He hated the "O" word. When he was told to sit, he argued, "I don't want to sit." When he was taught to stay, he complained, "I don't want to stay. I want to go with you; besides, I need a fire hydrant." He said, "I hate the 'O' word. One day my master made me stay so long that it happened—I made a puddle in front of the poodle, and I was mortified. I hate the 'O' word."

That's about the way I was feeling that day. I told everyone to keep their heads bowed and that no one was to look around. I didn't want anyone to see me leave the platform and go pray for this deceased lady. In obedience to God, I gingerly laid the microphone down so as not to draw attention to myself and quietly slipped up the aisle. I walked through the swinging doors into the lobby where my dear sister lay on the floor. I slowly approached the body. The doctor informed me as if I didn't already know, "This lady has passed, and no one is allowed in here." I pretended I didn't hear him—Mike says this is one of my gifts.

I considered going to her face, but chose instead to stop at her ankles. I guess it was a little less intimidating than the other end. I placed both hands on her ankles—expecting nothing—and said, "Lord, You told me to do this."

Now God knew He had told me to pray for this lady, but I wanted the doctor to know that God had told me to pray. Besides, if one says, "God told me," who can argue with that? If they deemed me a flake, at least I was a radically-saved flake!

So, I proceeded, "You, Lord, are the Resurrection and Life, and one day this lady will be raised from the dead in resurrection power. If You want to do that today, that would be great."

As I prayed this wimpy prayer out of sheer obedience to the voice of God, I looked up and saw the woman's eyes began to flutter. Right then, at that very moment, I knew God was going to raise her up, and we would see a miracle. I stood up, straightened my dress, wiped the tears from my face, squared my shoulders, and reentered the sanctuary with renewed vigor.

I could feel the strength of the Lord flowing through me. I retrieved the microphone and said, "I want to sing a song."

If looks could kill, I would be dead. I knew what they were thinking, *"You've already killed one person. Are you going for two?"* I didn't look at their faces. There was a supernatural presence empowering me. My music started.

First Verse:
A hand of fear gripped the crowd
that day at Jarius' home
When the doctor shook his head
and said, "She's gone."

You feel the mother's heartbreak;
you could hear her cry and mourn,
For her little girl was only twelve years old.
Then somewhere in the distance
outlined against the sun,
There came a man on a mission
from the throne.
They said, "Somebody's coming,"
but what they did not know
It was a promise coming down that dusty road.

Chorus:
There's a promise coming down that dusty road.
In His holy hands healing virtue flows.
He's got the key to what you need,
Death and hell He will defeat
For there's a promise
coming down that dusty road.

Second Verse:
Wonder turned to mocking
when Jesus did speak,
He said, "Your daughter's not dead.
She's just asleep."
Then He turned to unbelievers
and He told them to go home,
"Leave Me and death alone."

Then He laid His hand upon the child,
And He looked death right in the eye,

And said, "All power in heaven and earth
is given unto Me."
And with a voice that sounded like thunder
He hurled death asunder
And said, "Little girl, rise and be healed."[3]

At the very moment that I said, "Rise and be healed," the nurse let out a scream and exploded through the swinging doors at the rear of the auditorium like a rocket propelled grenade! She was screaming and saying, "She's alive! She's alive! She's alive!"

I was later told that when I sang, "He hurled death asunder and said, 'Rise and be healed,' " the dear lady sat straight up and then stood up. She was completely healed by the power of the resurrected Christ! She walked into the ambulance and allowed herself to be taken to the hospital. I suppose it was to prove that she was really alive—you know how the medical people can be. However, there was no sign of heart failure.

I talked to this dear retired missionary wife six years later, and she was still very much alive and living in Arizona.

With my personality, had I known what God was going to do that day, I would have carried my microphone into the lobby with me and commanded strongly for her to get up. How dare she die in my service! I still chuckle over the thought of that scene.

I doubt that anyone was able to absorb much after all that had transpired; nevertheless, I ended the service with a powerful message on "Lying Spirits." I certainly didn't need to preach on miracles or the resurrection, as the Holy Spirit had already put an exclamation mark on those topics. I will say that the service was no longer dead! There was no need to try to work up praise. The ladies left singing and praising God.

When the service finally concluded and everyone had gone, I gathered my things together, and feeling released from my fast, decided to go out for dinner- just Jesus and me. I didn't feel abandoned by the ladies, or alone, but I was in the company of Royalty.

I was hungry for steak. Cruising the highway, I saw a sign compelling folks to the restaurant. Its steak picture caused my glands to salivate. I turned into the crowded parking lot. First, I could not find a parking place. "Help me, Lord, I'm tired." No longer had the words slipped over my lips than the first parking slot right by the door opened up. "Thank You, Lord," I whispered.

As I entered the crowded waiting area, I knew it would be a long wait. The gal taking names informed me that it would be maybe an hour or longer before she could seat me. When she asked how many were in my party, it took all my restraint not to say two. "Okay," I said imagining how good the food would taste to me, and seated myself among all the others in the waiting area. She turned on her heels and said, "Never mind: I have a place for you right now." I was excited and felt a little smug as I passed all the waiting people who eyed me curiously as if to say, *"Who do you think you are?"* What they did not know was that I was on a date with King Jesus, and He was treating me like a lady.

It was one of the most memorable nights of my life. Tears of pleasure pool in my eyes anytime I reflect on the evening. The steak was the best I've ever eaten to this day; and, no, it did not make me sick eating a big meal at the end of such a fast.

Obedience—obedience to the call to fast followed with obedience to the call to pray. I did not know, could not see what that week would hold, but I obeyed, and God did the impossible. Obedience and faith go hand in hand.

SAMBURU MIRACLE

One of the most unclouded examples of faith I've ever witnessed took place in the jagged, rugged, dry wilderness near the humble community of Maralal in the territory of the Samburu tribe of Kenya. It had taken us two days of travel on the unforgiving barabara (Swahili for roads). These consisted of everything from rock-strewn trails that break shocks and threaten to shake the teeth from your head, to dry riverbeds laden with sand that threatens to suck you down any moment and hold you for the entire night. One stretch was a couple of hours of travel that simulated driving on an old-fashioned rub board.

Weary and road worn, we arrived at an archaic wood-planked lodge, which at one time more than fifty years earlier, may have had some class to it. But that ambiance had long-since faded away much like "Delta Dawn" in the fabled country song. It was the only game in town, so we checked in.

We showered in the slightly red/brown-colored water which reminded one of southern tea slightly too strong. It reeked with the aroma of mother earth and maybe just a hint of cesspool, but it actually felt refreshing if you talked to yourself just right. Certainly, it was better than no water at all, especially since the dusty roads made us look several shades darker before we washed the tan away.

The next hurdle to jump was much needed sleep, which has a way of dodging you when you're bone-weary. Dog-tired, I made an effort to rest in the undersized bed tightly covered with a mosquito net. Whiffs of ancient dust rammed into my sinuses like a runaway freight train. "Okay, girlie, you have two choices. Stay under the claustrophobic net and suffer allergies, or sleep out from under the net and become munchies for all the mosquitoes." I chose the net.

Hot coffee, toast with jam, and a roaring fire in the dining room gave us the impetus to start the new day. We drove to a valley about an hour away that had no hint of sophisticated amenities, but was nonetheless beautiful in an undeveloped frontier sort of way. We found a school that was not in use at the time, and acquired permission from the tribal elders to set up a medical clinic and preach the gospel.

Mike was outside the classrooms ministering the Word to the many people who had come to be seen by our medical staff—Dr. Jim, Dr. Ellen, and a couple of registered nurses. Dr. Jim, now in his sixties—a brilliant, kindhearted doctor with compassion oozing from his demeanor, a wonderful man—has devoted his life to the medical profession. Dr. Ellen—a credit to the female gender—is a bright, young, gifted doctor with a heart to help the helpless. She involves herself in medical mission clinics around the world. With these two great physicians on board, we felt like we could tackle just about anything thrown our way. However, that was about to change.

Toward the end of the day a beautiful young Samburu woman, who had patiently waited her turn, stepped inside the classroom and sat in the examination chair. The doctor asked, "How can we help you today?"

She was wearing a *shuka*, a solid piece of cloth that the Samburu and Maasai women use to cover their bodies in a wrap-around fashion. The lovely young woman said, "I've heard your God can do something about this." As she spoke, she opened her shuka revealing a gaping, bare, raw, open hole where her breast should have been. A moan escaped my lips as I peered at the putrefied flesh and meat around the exposed bone.

Doctor Jim looked at me and said with a soft compassionate spirit, "This dear, brave woman is in the final stages of cancer. It's already metastasized to the bone. She probably only has two weeks to live. There is nothing that we can do but give her pain medication and make her comfortable. It breaks my heart; she's so young. If only she could have gotten help sooner."

Her words were ringing in my ears: *"I've heard that your God can do something about this."*

"Jim," I said, "she has declared that our God can do something about her condition. She didn't come seeking medical help, but supernatural help. There *is* something that we can do! Pray!"

Mike came from where he had been preaching outside, and we called all the clinic stations to a halt. After explaining to everyone this precious lady's desperate plight, we laid hands on her and prayed a simple prayer. "Father, she believes that You can do something about her situation. Honor her faith."

When we finished praying this straightforward prayer, Mike explained the way of salvation to her, and she surrendered her heart to the Lord. We packed the medical supplies and departed from the area.

Months later, the secretary-treasurer of Kenya was in that very place, and a beautiful, healthy woman approached him. She opened her shuka to reveal pristine, smooth, black skin over a once-gaping hole and said, "Tell those people that their God did something about this."

She was healed—made whole in body and spirit. She had heard the message of salvation and the healing power of God from others who had come to the clinic-crusade. So she came in simple faith, believing what we had declared to her friends. God saw her childlike faith and instantly healed her body and wrote her name in the book of life.

FAITH IS:

- Faith is a daring confidence in God to catch you when you jump. If you can see and know your future, then it is not faith but your own ability to rescue yourself. The just shall live by faith.

- Faith is the substance of things hoped for but the evidence of things not seen.

- Faith is the surrender of our personal desire so that His will be accomplished.

- Faith is a relationship. A trust relationship with God, our cCreator, fully believing, completely persuaded, thoroughly convinced that He knows you by name and loves you more than you love yourself.

During my first bout with cancer, God gave me these following truths concerning faith.

TEN COMMANDMENTS OF FAITH

1. Thou Shalt Not Fear

2 Timothy 1:7 NKJV,
For God has not given us the spirit of fear but of power and of love and of a sound mind.

This Scripture indicates that fear is a spirit, and that God does not give us this spirit. This causes me to know that Satan is the one who gives us the spirit of fear. Fear is a tool he uses to cripple, hinder, and manipulate us. The Word says in the book of Luke that men's hearts will fail them for fear.

My mom was fond of saying, "Ninety-eight percent of what you fear will never happen."

I have always told my children, "Don't cross a bridge before you get to it."

Fear is an unhealthy enemy.

Even when the world becomes shaken, and the seas and the waves roar, and we know calamity is coming upon the earth; Jesus said, *"Look up, lift up your heads; for your redemption draws nigh."* Luke 21:28 KJV

> Isaiah 41:10 NASU,
> *"Do not fear, for I am with you;*
> *Do not anxiously look about you, for I am*
> *your God.*
> *I will strengthen you, surely I will help you,*
> *Surely I will uphold you with My righteous*
> *right hand."*

God gives us a command to not be afraid, for He is with us. He is telling us not to be discouraged, for He is our God, our Strength, and our Victor.

When God is with us, who can stand against us? This battle of fear is first fought on the battleground of the mind. It is there that we win or lose, *for as a man thinks in his heart so is he.* This is one of the reasons we must guard what we listen to, taste, and watch, for these are the doors that open into the fertile soil of the heart and mind.

2. Thou Shall Not Say, "I Am Weak"

> Joel 3:10 NKJV,
> *"Let the weak say I am strong."*

From the abundance of the heart the mouth speaks. If you feel you are weak and defeated, and you continually speak of being weak and defeated, then you will soon be weak and defeated.

> Psalm 27:1 NKJV,
> *The Lord is the strength of my life: of whom shall I be afraid?*

> 2 Corinthians 12:9 NKJV,
> *"My strength is made perfect in weakness."*

Jesus is trying to show us that His unlimited strength is made perfect in us during our time of human weakness.

More times than I can count, I've entered the pulpit sick with fever from some virus making its rounds and weak in body; nevertheless, when I stood to minister the Word, my symptoms departed, and I knew God was making His strength perfect in me. Some of the greatest services of which I have been a part were when I was at my worst.

3. Thou Shalt Not Talk of Inabilities

> Philippians 4:13 NKJV,
> *I can do all things through Christ which strengthens me.*

This is one of my favorite thoughts because this Scripture does not say, "If you are a man or a woman, if you are black or white, or if you are beautiful; it simply says, "*I can. . . .*" It does not even say, "I might be able to or if all things are favorable." It says, "*I can do all things. . . .*" It does not say "s*ome* things" but "*all things. . . .*" *All* is an infinitely inclusive word like *everything* or *nothing.* These words leave no room for doubt. The remainder of this Scripture explains why we can do all things. Through Jesus Christ, we can do all things. In ourselves we can do very little and would fail more times than succeed, but through Him, with Him, by Him working inside of us, strengthening us, causing us to succeed, we can do *"all things"*; therefore, we don't depend on our abilities, but His.

"If it'd been a rope, I'd a made it!"

Mikey, our son, was visiting his grandparents when he was just a little boy. He moved a floor lamp to the second story window, and proceeded to climb out of the window with the help of the lamps electrical cord. The cord was only about six feet long—not nearly long enough to reach the ground. My dad heard him cry when he hit the stony surface with a thud. Dad ran out to see just what had happened. Mikey looked up with skinned knees and hands, and said, "If it'd been a rope, I'd made it"!

Faith is when you trust God without the rope to hold on to.

4. Thou Shall Not Talk of Pain and Feelings of Sickness, or Be Afraid of Pain or Sickness

> Matthew 8:17 NKJV,
> *Himself took our infirmities and bore our sickness.*

> Isaiah 53:5 NKJV,
> *By His stripes we are healed.*

> Exodus 15:26 KJV,
> *I am the Lord that healeth thee.*

Not only did Jesus take our sins and transgressions to the cross, but He also took our sicknesses and infirmities. Because of Him, everything is possible; nothing is impossible with Him. I have personally witnessed Him open blinded eyes, unstop deaf ears, restore crippled bodies, and heal incurable diseases.

I remember an incident that occurred during an outdoor crusade in Kenya. There were over eleven thousand in attendance that afternoon. A lady came to the meeting, creeping along with the help of a crude wooden walking stick. From the platform, I had noticed the old woman when she first hobbled into the crowd. Hundreds responded to the salvation altar call, and among them was this crippled woman. After the prayer of salvation was given, Mike made a second call for the sick and afflicted, stating, "God not only made provision for our sins, but our sicknesses as well." The crippled woman also responded to this call. When God touched her, she threw down her cane and began to shout for joy. After some time had passed she bent over, picked up her stick, stuck it in her back sack, and walked away leaping and praising God for all that He had done in her life.

Exodus 23:25 KJV,
I will take sickness from the midst of thee

5. Thou Shalt Not Worry or Be Anxious

Philippians 4:6-7 KJV,
Be careful for nothing but in every thing by prayer and supplication with thanksgiving let your request be made known unto God. And the peace of God, which passeth all understanding, shall keep your hearts and minds through Christ Jesus.

Verse 8,
Whatsoever things are true, whatsoever things are honest, whatsoever things are just, whatsoever things are pure, whatsoever things are lovely, whatsoever things are of good report; if there be any virtue, and if there be any praise, think on these things.

1 Peter 5:7 KJV,
Casting all your cares upon him, for he careth for you.

6. Thou Shalt Not Fear Poverty

Philippians 4:19-20 NKJV,
And my God shall supply all your need according to His riches in glory by Christ Jesus. Now to our God and Father be glory forever and ever. Amen.

Psalm 37:25 NASU,
I have been young and now I am old, Yet I have not seen the righteous forsaken Or his descendants begging bread.

Psalm 23:1 NASU,
The Lord is my shepherd, I shall not want.

3 John 1:2 NKJV,
Beloved, I pray that you may prosper in all things.

Psalm 1:3 NASU,
He will be like a tree firmly planted by streams of water, Which yields its fruit in its season And its leaf does not wither; And in whatever he does, he prospers.

7. Thou Shalt Not Be Terrified by Trouble or Any Evil

Isaiah 54:17 NASB,
"No weapon that is formed against you will prosper;
And every tongue that accuses you in judgment you will condemn.
This is the heritage of the servants of the Lord,
And their vindication is from Me," declares the Lord.

Psalm 23:4 NKJV,
Yea, though I walk through the valley of the shadow of death, I will fear no evil;
For You are with me;

2 Timothy 4:18 NKJV,
And the Lord will deliver me from every evil work and preserve me for His heavenly kingdom. To Him be glory forever and ever. Amen!

8. Thou Shalt Not Fear Persecution

Matthew 5:10 NASB,
Blessed are those who have been persecuted for the sake of righteousness, for theirs is the kingdom of heaven.

Romans 8:28-29 NKJV,
And we know that all things work together for good to those who love God, to those who are the called according to His purpose.

Romans 8:35-36 NKJV,
Who shall separate us from the love of Christ? Shall tribulation, or distress, or persecution, or famine, or nakedness, or peril, or sword?

Romans 8:37-39 NKJV,
Yet in all these things we are more than conquerors through Him who loved us. For I am persuaded that neither death nor life, nor angels nor principalities nor powers, nor things present nor things to come, nor height nor depth, nor any other created thing, shall be able to separate us from the love of God which is in Christ Jesus our Lord.

9. Thou Shalt Not be Afraid of Men or Demons

1 John 4:4-5 NASB,
You are from God, little children, and have overcome them; because greater is He who is in you than he who is in the world.

Matthew 10:28-29 NASB,

*Do not fear those who kill the body but are
unable to kill the soul; but rather fear Him
who is able to destroy both soul and body in
hell.*

Luke 10:19 NASB,

*Behold, I have given you authority to tread
on serpents and scorpions, and over all the
power of the enemy, and nothing will injure
you.*

10. Thou Shalt Not Be in Doubt Regarding God's Guidance

Psalm 37:23 NKJV,

*The steps of a good man are ordered by the
Lord,
And He delights in his way.*

Proverbs 3:5-6 NASB,

*Trust in the Lord with all your heart
And do not lean on your own understanding.
In all your ways acknowledge Him,
And He will make your paths straight.*

John 16:13 NASB,

*But when He, the Spirit of truth, comes, He
will guide you into all the truth;*

God's Spirit will never lead you where His grace cannot keep you.

---

*Never doubt in the dark
what God has told you
in the light.*

9
FIRE ON THE ISLAND

Zanzibar

9
FIRE ON THE ISLAND

Zanzibar

Wind-blown and smelling of the warm salt air, we dragged our few belongings with us. Making our way past the ancient port of call, we could feel history coming alive as we walked up the old wooden planks leading us from the modern hydrofoil water-ferry to Stone Town, Zanzibar, an island off the coast of Tanzania, Africa. I could easily imagine myself with shipmasters a hundred years earlier—seeing the same sights, hearing the same sounds, and watching the unloading of their cargo from the ships onto the flats in the ancient warehouse.

The two-hour boat ride from the mainland of Dar es Salaam, Tanzania was rough, and I was personally thankful I had kept down my recently eaten meal in spite of my queasy stomach.

As we disembarked at Zanzibar, the air was warm and thick. Local *hawkers* approached, eager to provide hotels, restaurants, and transportation. I marveled at the rich shades of their mahogany skin. "This way, Mista!" "Welcome, Madame (pronounced Mud 'em). Welcome!"

Immediately we noticed a seawall on this side of the island that kept the water back at high tide. Scantily dressed young boys jumped off the wall into the Indian Ocean, swam some distance to a place where they could scale the wall, and then climbed back to repeat the action. All the while, water pounded furiously against the seawall, sending spray high into the air. About ten feet in from the wall, were pots of boiled, fried, and grilled seafood—ranging from lobster to shrimp and everything else imaginable. During our time there, I became especially fond of the grilled lobster. It was quite the festive atmosphere as people walked along the seaside eating, drinking, and making merriment.

The sights and sounds of Zanzibar made us think that we had stepped back into the days of David

Livingstone, the great missionary-explorer who had used this place as the starting point of his expeditions to the mainland.

Strolling leisurely among the many busy open markets, I was enthralled with the unique beauty of the island, the colorful cloths, smells of the fresh seafood cooking, and was deeply moved by the lack of knowledge of the saving power of Jesus.

I knew that Mike was feeling the same when he turned to our missionary area field director and asked, "Why can't we have a crusade here, friend?"

His surprising response was, "There are four reasons why you can't. One, it is a one-hundred-percent Muslim island, and you'll never get permission. Two, even if you did, it would be in an obscure location where no one would know where you were. Three, no one would come; and four, if they did come, it would be to stone you." I think he thought with this declaration as the old saying goes, "That was that." What he, nor we, could know was at that very moment "The Ancient of Days" was rolling up His sleeve because He had other plans and those plans involved us. After all, His Son died for these people.

The streets were busy with donkey-drawn carts, man-drawn taxies—rickshaws, and a few old, open-bed trucks called, "dolla-dolla." This name began when rides were offered for a dollar. However, it costs much more than a dollar today. Wanting to see the entire island, we decided to ride for a while. Ducking our heads to avoid a nasty knot from the overhead rails, we climbed into the back of an open *dolla-dolla*.

As we continued our ride on the *dolla-dolla* to our hotel, we noted that cars could be driven only on the main street. Most of the streets were barely wide enough for a *piki-piki*—motorbike. The buildings were tall with small windows. Their entrances were large wooden carved doors with ornate brass fittings. Physiologically, this made it hard for me to breathe. It was dusty and dirty. Ladies, dressed in all black with just a narrow slit for their eyes, roamed the streets and alleys. I wondered how they kept from suffocating in the sticky heat, or from stepping in front of something and being killed. It was heartbreaking to me. I wanted to reach them with the good news that Jesus loves them.

We spent the night in one of the tall, narrow hostels. We climbed a circular staircase that seemingly wound its way into the stratosphere just to reach our tiny bedroom at the top. In true Zanzibar fashion, the bed had a high wooden carved headboard and matching footboard with designs of the sheiks' castles expertly carved into the grain. A small Persian rug lay beside the bed in the sparsely decorated room.

The next morning we enjoyed our breakfast on the roof of the hotel in the breezy salt air, overlooking the city of Stone Town where 300,000 souls in desperate need of Jesus resided. As we finished our wonderful meal—delicious fruit, eggs, and fresh baked bread—we began to reflect upon our knowledge of this island and its mysterious and quaint environs.

Zanzibar simultaneously silences and thrives on its checkered past. It is part of Tanzania, yet autonomous; a land constantly squabbled over by abolitionists, unscrupulous slave traders, and pirates. "The past is never dead; it's not even past," reads the sign hanging above the Zanzibar National Archives. Never truer words, especially in the case of Zanzibar! The land is heavy with history. Mike, being a history buff, was enthralled with the place, as only a student of the past could understand, for truly here was history come to life. The environs of Zanzibar have changed very little over several centuries.

The world-renowned explorers—Livingstone, Speke, and Burton—all used Zanzibar as a springboard for their travels. Its historical fame for the selling of slaves and piracy gives it both a colorful past and present.

The Mangapwani Slave Caves, the Anglican Cathedral, and the slave market of Stone Town saw huge numbers of slaves captured both by local African leaders delivering enemies from battle, and by Arab traders.

Known as the shortest war in history, the Anglo-Zanzibar War of 1896 lasted all of 38 minutes. Today the only reminder is the cannon, which sits sedately outside the House of Wonders.

The natives from the mainland of Tanzania were captured and sent to Bagamoya—known as *the place of the crushed heart*. To this day in Bagamoya, you can feel the spirit of hopelessness in the air. From Bagamoya, the captured slaves were brought to Zanzibar Island and hidden in underground caverns. Zanzibar was the last stop before the slave ships were launched to regions beyond across the ocean.

In Zanzibar, there is a dungeon beneath the slave market headquarters consisting of a small four-foot by eight-foot hole dug into the wall. It has one tiny opening for air, and a trough for the seawater to come in at high tide to wash out the human waste. It is inconceivable to put anyone in this dark hole. Certainly no more than ten could sit on the cement shelves on either side of the dungeonesque room. However, they did not place ten on these two two-by-eight-foot shelves, but ninety poor desperate souls.

Many suffocated to death, leaving only the strong to face the long haul across open seas. The survivors were sold in a market like cattle at an auction.

Mothers had babies torn from their arms and slaughtered at a place that resembled a birdbath. Babies were of no use to slave traders, so they would brutally chop off their heads with their scimitars and throw them in a pit at *The Place of Slaughter*. I could not contain my tears as images of humans chained like dogs, beaten and butchered if it suited the fancy of their Muslim captors, assaulted my vision, crushing my heart and mind.

At the *House of Wonders*, some of the Arabs would sight in their guns by having a slave climb a tree. If they had it sighted correctly, there would be one less slave for sale. It was all so barbaric. Our guide told us that slaves were beheaded, and the heads were buried in the cement base of each pillar that surrounds the *House of Wonder*, a magnificent whitewashed mansion on the sea— one head for each pillar.

David Livingstone was so distressed over the inhumanity to his fellow human beings that he single-handedly, and I might add, successfully, put a stop to the slave trade on this island, at least on the surface. Later, an Anglican church was built over the hellhole, which had been the slave market. The high altar in this church had been the whipping post where the African captives had gone through the most brutal treatment to see who was the strongest to bring the highest price. The infant baptismal tank was located over the pit where the bodies of headless infants were thrown like garbage simply because there was no profit for the cruel slave traders.

When we left the island, our hearts were heavy because of the past suffering and the present spiritual darkness. Zanzibar became one of the top places on our prayer list.

Three months later, we returned to Zanzibar with the area directors of that time. As we exited the boat ramp and boarded a *dolla-dolla*, Mike turned with a start ready to fight when a perfect stranger grabbed his shoulder. (My husband was strung as a guitar string tightened two pitches too high because a thief had attacked him in a place on the mainland called Bagamoya, causing him to have to fight for his belongings. He was just a little more than jumpy. All this had occurred only a few days before.) Mike turned around, ready to take purpose, when the man held up a poster inviting people to our crusade in Dar es Salaam. He said, "Will you do this on this island?" Mike replied, "Brother, you know we would love to, but you know we would never get permission from this government." God never ceases to amaze us, when He shows His love for lost souls.

When old Tanganyika and Zanzibar combined as Tanzania, the new constitution required that if the country had a Muslim as president for ten years, then it must have a non-Muslim one for the same amount of time. Unknown to us, that change had just occurred. The young man God had chosen to pioneer a work on the island said, "I want to introduce you to someone." He proceeded to introduce us to the assistant to the new president of Tanzania for Zanzibar—an elder in the

Assemblies of God on the mainland. That man looked at Mike and said, "You have permission to preach here anywhere you wish!"

Mike turned to our mission's director for Tanzania and said, "What about it, boss?"

He replied, "This is the invitation for which we have waited 130 years! Yes, you have our permission."

That day, as we walked along the stone wall built to keep back high tidewaters, ate grilled fish out on the streets, and looked at the unsaved people of Zanzibar, my heart soared within me, for I felt a change was coming. God had opened a door for the gospel to be preached on this one-hundred-percent Muslim island!

We spent the next three months praying and preparing to preach the first evangelical crusade on Zanzibar—actually the first overt Christian witness in 130 years!

Back in the United States, people began to call, wanting to join us for ministry in Zanzibar. We half-jestingly said, "Don't come unless you are ready to die. We have no idea what will happen when we start to preach. They may stone us, or we may have revival."

One morning the jingling of the house phone interrupted our reverie. Mike took the last swig of his coffee and answered.

"Morning, Mike," said a missionary friend from Tanzania.

"Morning to you. I guess it's actually evening for you guys. What's up?"

"We have an opportunity that is too good to pass up. When Livingstone fought to stop slavery, property was given in his honor to bury Christians on the island of Zanzibar. Over the years, it's turned into an impromptu place for the discarding of refuse. The Muslim government has threatened to take this burial site back and give it to squatters, unless the Anglican Church (with an island presence in name only) builds a seven-foot stonewall around the property. This would cost $7,000. As you know, the Anglican building constructed over the slave market is nothing more than a museum, as there are no Anglicans on the island. Their representative has offered it to the brother who asked you to preach on the island. It goes without saying that he has no money."

According to history, in about 1860 Dr. David Livingstone made another of his forays into the

African mainland. When he arrived in Zambia, he discovered a thief had stolen his medical kit. Quinine he used to cure malaria was in that kit. He contracted the disease and died. It is said that when they found him, his body was in the position of prayer by his bed. Because of the great love the African bearers had for him, and knowing of his love for Africa, they buried his heart under a tree. They then made a litter to carry his body, and bore it many weeks back to Zanzibar. Out of gratitude, the Church of England gave these men some property in the middle of nowhere. These men did not know what to do with it, so they made it a place to bury Christians on this Muslim island.

Unknown to us at this time, that land was in the heart of the largest housing development in Stone Town. The *Ancient of Days* had rolled up His sleeves. He was at work from eternity, but in this case 130 years prior!!!

The friend who had called continued, "I have $4,000. Can you come up with $3,000? If you can, we will buy this property, sight unseen, and you'll at least have a place to preach your crusade. The site will be deeded to the Tanzania Assemblies of God."

Mike didn't hesitate. "Yes, I'll come up with the money somehow." And, by God's grace, we did.

We landed on Zanzibar for the third time, and made our way to the property. Having no idea just what we had purchased, we could hardly contain our excitement as we were about to view this plot for the first time. Mike and I looked at each other in utter shock, not knowing whether to laugh or cry. We witnessed a miracle, because the Muslims have full control of the island.

Tears pooled in our eyes as we stood by the graves of people who had died of the fever at young ages—some 20 years old, others 22 or 23—missionaries who came 130 years before us.

Mike and I joined hands and bowed our heads in reverence for people who had come with high hopes and dreams. Some of them lasted only a year, but each one became the seed for the harvest that would begin 130 years later. Mike quietly said, "With the help of the Holy Spirit, we will endeavor to finish what you started." It was altogether sobering. We felt the heavy weight of responsibility because of their sacrifice.

The property we had purchased was the only bare piece of ground in the midst of scores of apartment buildings and houses, and was the size of two football fields. How can anyone ever doubt God's concern for souls when one sees His ordering of events for such a long a period of time? We knew that we were on this island of Zanzibar by divine appointment from the Almighty to bring the good news of salvation.

Rather than holding our crusade behind the stone walls where people might feel uncomfortable to attend, Mike erected a platform on the fairgrounds across from the largest mosque on Zanzibar.

We set up our public address system and began the music. A few began gathering, then a few more, until we had by head count of over 150. Remember: this is an all-Muslim island.

Music is an incredible universal tool to draw in a crowd. Almost immediately, the mosque began its chant to Allah over a PA system, which Mike calls the voice of the devil. My husband began praying that their huge horn speakers would not drown us out, but Yahweh did better than that. He broke their system instantly, and it stayed that way for the entire week of the crusade! The imams came down out of their tower—at least five of them—with their arms folded and angry. I thought the people might run away, but they remained.

After Mike brought the Word and a few came forward to publicly accept Jesus, the imams called him aside and said, "We want to debate you about Jesus."

Mike responded, "I have not come here to debate. I came to preach Jesus Christ and Him crucified. If you believe Him, you can go to heaven. If you reject Him, you will spend eternity in a lake of fire."

They said, "Humph," turned, and walked away.

As the second night of crusade proceeded, much to our surprise, there were over 300 gathered in the open fairgrounds to hear the music and message that followed. A few more came to Jesus.

On the third night, 500 curious souls came, along with a line of sullen imams—arms folded. On this night, after the music and the ministry of the Word, Mike called for the sick to be brought forward for prayer. A grandmother brought a nine-year-old girl named Happy, who was deaf from birth. Mike laid hands on the child, prayed a simple prayer, and her deafness was instantly and completely healed!

A Muslim lady, dressed in the full black Islamic attire with only her eyes revealing any sign of flesh, was brought forward for prayer. Her legs were crippled. Mikey, our son, knelt down, and laid hands on her knees. Instantly, she was healed!

A young boy who had been dropped on his head as a baby, suffering brain damage, which left him unable to walk or speak, was lifted up to the platform. Mike and I laid our hands on him and prayed a simple prayer. God instantly healed the boy, and he began to walk, run, and speak!

Two hundred sixty-seven people converted from Islam to Christianity.

The imams again cornered Mike. However, this time was different. With tears in their eyes, they said, "We don't want to debate you anymore about Jesus. We just want to hear what you have to say."

We went to Zanzibar expecting a possible stoning. Instead, the Rock, Christ Jesus, was glorified by a mighty move of the Holy Spirit!

Two mud churches were birthed from of the main stone church, which was built on the cemetery site. Some time later, we returned to the island to preach a round-robin revival in the three locations. Because of a communication breakdown outside of our ministry, we could not obtain a permit for an outdoor crusade, so, Mike,

Mikey, and I rotated preaching at the different locations simultaneously. Sometimes, even in the game of life, you have to punt. We believe that God causes all things to work together for His good, and this was no exception. All three churches were packed with standing room only, and outsiders looking through the windows. God sent another incredible move of His Spirit with amazing signs and wonders!

A young imam who had been trained for Islamic service in Pakistan had just come to the island for their form of evangelism. He had been walking all across the island, encouraging people in their Islamic faith, and he happened to meet one of our new pastors of the mud church. He began to talk to the pastor about Islam, but all the pastor could do was tell this gentleman about more than twenty significant miracles that had occurred while Mikey was preaching there this very week.

Our pastor was so excited he could not stop talking. The imam was so overwhelmed by what he heard, all he could say was, "I want to be saved!"

The pastor thought that he had misheard, so he responded, "You what?"

"I want to be saved."

The pastor, being somewhat of a novice, innocently said, "You will have to go down to the main church for that."

This had taken place on a Saturday afternoon. That evening, as I was preparing to bring the Word at the main church, I was unaware of the pending guest. God burned into my heart a message of His deity called, "I Am He."

A special anointing was present in the service. To our astonishment, at the end of the ministry time, our pastor escorted the Pakistani imam to the platform. The Islamic leader informed us and the entire congregation that he wanted to become a Christian. He knelt in front of the crowd, and Mike led him in the sinner's prayer. It was just incredible!

Zanzibar is one of the greatest missionary stories of this century. I am so thankful that God chose us to be a small part in His great plan.

Zanzibar was a God-thing! Zanzibar is no longer one hundred percent Muslim. At last count, there were eight Assemblies of God churches on the island.

I may never walk the streets of Zanzibar again, but I will not in any way forget the wonderful things that God did there.

10
RESCUED TO TRIUMPH

A Word From the Author

10
RESCUED TO TRIUMPH

A Word From the Author

Those who have no battles are DEAD! We who dwell in the land of the living are continually faced with trials and tribulations. These trials are not meant to destroy us, but only make us stronger. Yet, our response to these trials can destroy us.

I will actually take it a step further, and say that I believe God allows us to go through trials so that He may be glorified in the land of the living.

As long as there is breath in your body, there will be pain, tribulation, trials, hurt, victories, and healing. It's all a part of living and life.

We have all felt abandoned and alone at one time or another; existing, breathing, and moving out of habitual routine. We have had the feeling that at any moment the quicksand of life would swallow us whole as we trudge through the sticky, miry clay, unable to escape its muddy pull; falling and being sucked down into the depths of despair-forever its captive. Just because we are children of the King does not mean that we are immune to these feelings. However, when we find ourselves in trouble, the Spirit of God who dwells within us encourages us to believe that Jehovah is working on our behalf.

Life can seem to spin out of control and become overwhelming, as in many of the stories that I have shared with you. When I feel Satan as that evil roaring lion seeking to devour my soul and conniving to make me his next victim, the Deliverer out of Zion, the GREAT I AM and my Lord, opens my eyes to a mental picture of the

Lion of the Tribe of Judah rising up behind me. He roars a roar of protection and defense that sends all imps of hell running in fear with their tails tucked between their legs. I am left alone in the comfort of the King.

The book of Revelation declares that the Lion of the Tribe of Judah has triumphed. This Lion of heaven has paid the ultimate price and has rescued us from Satan's prowl.

He did not create you to fail.

The weapons of our warfare are not carnal weapons, but they are mighty. You could call them "secret weapons" because the world cannot see them. They are omnipotent to the pulling down of the strongholds in our lives.

This one thing I know. We, as believers, win in life and death. The only thing we have to fear is fear itself. Our days were numbered in our mother's womb and, until God is finished with us, we are immortal. We do not want to be here a day longer than what He has ordered. If we are not afraid of dying, what is there to fear? We know these principles, and yet our humanity wars against them. I do understand these wars all too well.

SPARED, *Chronicles of the Call: Book 2* will feature the testimony of Mikey's burn and many more adventure stories from world travels. You don't want to miss this volume as we share with you the power of the living God to deliver His children in the face of danger, suffering, and certain death.

ENDNOTES

[1]Heath, J. L., Composer. (1918) Wells, James, Lyrics. (1918). *Living by Faith. Public Domain*

[2]Huff, David. One Less Stone [Recorded by Marigold Cheshier]. On *Got the Spirit* [CD] Christian World, 1995

[3]Phillips, Randy. (1988). Promise [Recorded by Marigold Cheshier]. On *Got the Spirit* [CD] Christian World, 1995

ABOUT THE AUTHOR

Marigold Cheshier is the most extraordinary person I know. Her talents run the gamut—from recording more than twenty solo music projects, preaching conferences and conventions all around the world (her travels have now taken her to more than 80 countries of the world), to television ministries such as PTL, TBN, as well as many local stations, and serving as a busy pastor's wife in several great churches.

She and her husband now serve as missionary-evangelists in the country of Kenya, running orphanages, and building churches among the Maasai people, having planted more than 120 churches through evangelism. All of this ministry began when she was only 12 years old.

Marigold is a mother of two great children—a son, James Michael Cheshier, and a daughter, Melissa Jeanet White. She is grandmother to twin grandsons, Michael and Maurice White; a granddaughter, Serenity Cheshier; and a third grandson, the youngest of her grandchildren, Gabriel Cheshier. Both of her children are in the ministry. Her son, "Mikey," is a pastor in Monroe, Louisiana; and daughter, Melissa, is an extremely successful children's pastor and evangelist. All the grandchildren also say they will be involved in missions in some form or another.

In this day of "extreme this and extreme that or the other," Marigold is a woman of extreme faith. She was given up to die in 1982. The attending doctor told her and me that she had 18 months to live during a bout with breast cancer. There have been a number of other life-threatening situations from which she has emerged victorious.

For years, many have told Marigold she needed to write a book. She always said that she was "too busy living it" to write it. Now, however, God has provided the opportunity for her to write her experiences for His glory. With that in view, it is a great joy to present *Rescued: The Chronicles of the Call Book 1*. This work comes from the pen of one of the most loving and compassionate people I know—all for the glory of God. I can say all this without fear of equivocation because I know her better than anyone does. I am her husband. I guarantee that you will weep and laugh as you read this book.

Mike Cheshier